ELEPHANT DANCE

Elephant Dance

By

FRANCES HUBBARD FLAHERTY

WITH A PREFACE BY
JOHN COLLIER

NEW YORK
CHARLES SCRIBNER'S SONS
1937

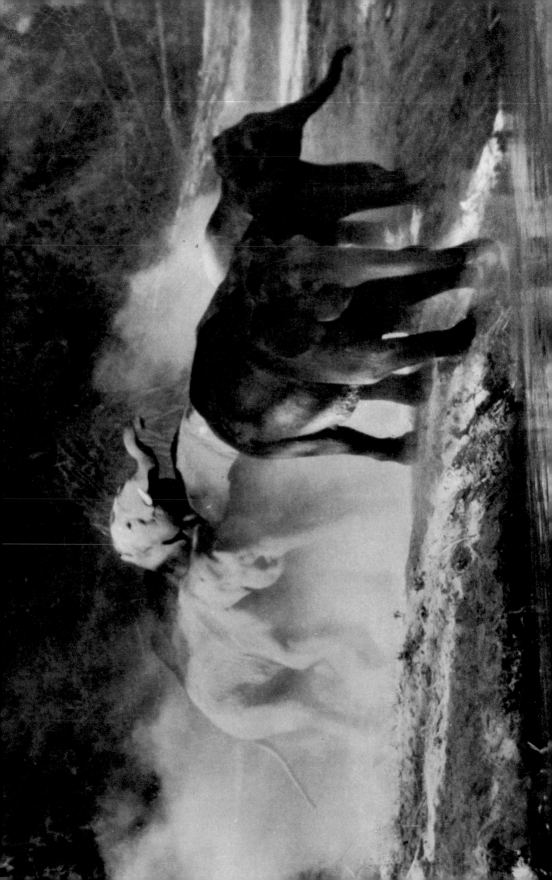

PREFACE

This kind of book—and it is a rare kind—is the best television we have yet discovered. It is scarcely a book at all. Never did print have such difficulty in remaining black or paper so nearly dissolve into a clear and Indian air. It would be absurd to discuss the writing as writing, as it would be to talk of the brushwork of a smile seen in the street.

In short, these letters are not works of art, but works of nature. Nature has certain advantages— naturalness among others. And for authenticity there is nothing to beat it, as those artists admit who marry their models.

So here we have India as one person saw it; the right sort of India and the right sort of person. No politics or ologies intrude; there are palaces, jungles, monkeys, elephants. That is the India I was brought up upon. A lot of people have been tinkering with it ever since, and I am to learn that it is still there beyond

5

[facing '. . . THE ELEPHANTS ARE GONE BACK TO THEIR JUNGLE'
Photograph by Barbara Flaherty van Ingen

the tropic ocean, and I am glad to have a piece of it here in my hand.

By good luck, which again belongs to nature, these casual letters tell a story, or at least follow its contour. The story is that of a Flaherty film. A Flaherty film differs from others; the making of it is an adventure rather than a gamble. It is an exploration into a sort of beauty that cannot be put 'under contract'.

These letters are a record of such an exploration, of a search for all that is most delightful and exciting in India. That must have been a great pleasure, and pleasure is the very stuff of which they are compounded. No wonder it is such a pleasure to read them.

JOHN COLLIER

CONTENTS

ILLUSTRATIONS

9

10

11

A WORD OF EXPLANATION

Lest there be any bothersome confusion about them, the members of the Flaherty family who will be met with in these letters are: my husband, 'Bob' or 'Daddy'—Robert Flaherty, producer of films; his brother and assistant, David Flaherty—'Uncle David'; our eldest daughter Barbara, 'Barbie', with us in India; and two younger daughters, Frances and Monica, at school in England most of the time, though they did come to India while we were there. These last are the 'Darlings' who were chiefly responsible for this spilling of ink.

The occasion for writing the letters was our making a film in Mysore, southern India. And how did we come to be making a film in southern India? Because of an idea we had had in mind for a number of years.

From the time, 1920, that my husband first began making films of Eskimos in Hudson Bay, we had spent the years making film expeditions to various corners of the globe,—to the South Seas, to Samoa and Tahiti, to the American desert where we tried to film the pueblo Indians but found them—alas—intractable, to some rocky islands off the coast of Ireland. . . . Wherever we took our camera, from one primitive scene to another, we used the native people as our characters and took our material from the stuff of their lives. We found what good actors native children can be, and how appealing they unfailingly are to an audience. So we had this idea;—why, if we wrote a film-story around extraordinary adventures that a native boy might have in his native environment, wouldn't it be possible to 'star' that boy himself in the film?

We set about to write a story. The first one we wrote was of a Spanish boy, and it was based on an actual happening—the pardoning by public acclaim of a famous Spanish fighting bull in the bull ring. Our story, following the adventures of the two together, developed the devotion of the boy for the bull up to his pride and agony in the final life-or-death scene. It was a good story. But we were uncertain of the bull; we were uncertain whether we could show a bull on the screen and make him so convincing in his lovability as to be sufficiently appealing and sympathetic. With what animal, we asked ourselves, would it be easier to do this? Why, of course, with that great lumbering, antediluvian pet, that greatest oddity and most peculiarly engaging of all God's creatures on earth—the elephant! Our story shifted instantly to India. What more intriguing than the adventures of a little Indian boy on a big Indian elephant in the jungles of India with all the jungle creatures?

But who could be found to produce such a film—a film that depended on a 'star' who was a mere boy, and a native boy at that, a quite ideal boy, moreover, who had yet to be discovered by some one of us somewhere in India! This needed a producer, it must be admitted, of no little courage and enterprise. Fortunately there was such a one in London. There was Alexander Korda. Almost before we realized it we found ourselves on his production schedule under the working title of 'Elephant Boy'.

But, Mr. Korda now remembered, there was already a famous story of a boy and an elephant that almost everybody knew—Kipling's *Jungle Book* story of 'Toomai of the Elephants'. Immediately the necessary arrangements were made between Mr. Korda and Mr. Kipling and the film rights to the character of 'Little Toomai' and of 'Kala Nag' and to the Kipling title were ours. And the rights to the Kipling story as well, of course, if we wished to use it. The Kipling story revolves about an Elephant dance—the 'dance' of wild elephants in the jungle at night. This was pure fantasy. Or was it somewhat fact? Was anyone suggesting that we should find—or make believe

—an Elephant dance in the jungles of India for our film?

Anyway our minds were full of other pressing and more practical questions. Where in all India should we go to make the film? To British India, or to a native state? Where, first of all, were the wild elephants? Most of them were way off in Assam, in remote jungles. But there were plenty too in the jungles of Mysore in south India, hardly 800 miles south of Bombay. Would His Highness, the Maharajah of Mysore, an exclusive and conservative ruler, be graciously disposed to let us work in his domain? Would he let us have his elephants? For we needed a quantity of tame elephants as well as wild ones.

With all these questions still in the air, my husband, with Barbara and David, set out for Bombay. By the time, six weeks later, that I was ready to follow them, all had been settled—settled by the gracious permission of H.H. the Maharajah of Mysore, by a telegram of welcome from his Dewan, Sir Mirza Ismail, and on the warm recommendation of His Excellency, Lord Willingdon, who said that he couldn't think of a better place for us to go.

PART I
MAY TO NOVEMBER

B

West End Hotel,
Bangalore, Mysore,
May 15th.

Darlings,

A VERY spiffy hotel and such a spiffy apartment *Arrival in*
as we have! Six rooms and a verandah for the two of *Bangalore*
us. It isn't done for us to share a dressing room and
bath, so we each have our own! (4) and bedroom
(shared!) (5) and sitting room (6). Drapery doors and
everything open, and the breeze blowing through.
The beds are netted. Got my first malaria inoculation,
i.e. mosquito bite. The brutes don't buzz, they simply
bite. Fans all buzzing; big ones hung from the ceiling
go round like a Dutch windmill. But it is *not hot.*
After Bombay and the boat it is deliciously cool.

Barbie met me in Bombay. The journey down was- *By Rail from*
n't half as bad as I had expected. There were great *Bombay to*
preparations in the way of fruit and lime squash and *Bangalore*

19

Evian water and two huge pails of ice. A first class compartment is a room all by itself; no corridor; with its own toilet and wash room, two big fans, two long leather settees. Barbara, like an old-timer, pulled out of her bedding roll a neat little woven rug which just fitted the seat, and there, *à la princess* we reclined behind closed shutters to keep out the sun, but with a crack open to look out on the country side as we rattled through it at a good European clip.

It was country like our desert country round Tucson,— very, very like. The earth is that lovely, soft, reddish-yellow colour. There are low bushy cactus and rows of that same Mexican cactus that is so picturesque, and there are many large, shapely, spreading trees of a deep luscious green. There were the same bouldery buttes rising out of the plain. There was the same sense of great space. But yet there was a greater delicacy about it. It wasn't wild and rude, it was beautifully refined and sweetly and subtly patterned and decorative. I could begin to understand the delicacy and subtlety of Indian design. And when, my dears, the Indian women and the bullock carts came into the picture, then, oh then, how I wished I could draw! Because I don't think I could possibly describe it.

Daddy met us in Bangalore, looking quite old-timerish too, in his topi, and completely wedded to Gul Kahn. Gul Kahn is his 'bearer'. Everybody has a bearer, or two or three. Anyway, you always have

20

[*facing* A PEASANT, A BULLOCK, A BUFFALO AND A BOWL OF RICE

Photograph by Barbara Flaherty van Ingen

one who is your body-servant—body-soul-and-purse servant as a matter of fact. He does everything for you but brush your teeth. I mean it. He is your shadow. You can't lose him from the time he comes in the morning to wake you and draw your bath until, having turned down your sheet and put out your slippers and tucked in the netting, he salaams a 'good night'. Then you can have yourself to yourself, for what's left of the evening!

Barbie and I had a bearer just to bring us from Bombay here. I wish you could have seen him. He has gone back to Bombay, so I can't even send a snap of him. He was a huge man, with a very splendid black beard and a splendid portly bearing, and a brilliant purple turban, which he wore, in the manner of his tribe in the north, with one end flowing down behind. I was scared to death of him, but Barbara carried him off superbly. She has quite the correct mem-sahib manner already.

Ameer (that was his name) rode in a third class compartment in a whole row of carriages overflowing with motley Indian humanity. At every stop his purple turban would come bobbing, towering above the station crowd, and he would stoop and peer in at the window, or suddenly appear in the doorway with his huge bulk. Was there anything we wanted? Would we have tea? Would we have our lunch in the station or brought into the compartment? He thought we

Ameer had better have it in the compartment. The next stop would be the one to get out and go to the dining car. Now he was going to fix our bedding, etc. I thought I'd die when Barbara had to ask this mountain of dignity for . . . toilet paper!

Daddy's bearer, Gul Kahn, is much travelled. His last sahib took him right round the world to—where do you suppose?—Mamaroneck, Connecticut (the station after Stamford, do you remember?). But Gul Kahn got homesick. His wages weren't American wages like the other servants'. The American children made fun of him.

He comes from Peshawar, up by the Khyber Pass, the toughest frontier town, Daddy says, in all the world. Besides a big wall, it has an electrified barbed-wire entanglement all around it. The gates are closed at six o'clock. The cinema audiences are guarded by police with fixed bayonets. Through the Pass, as through the opening in a dam, pour all the caravans from the north, north-east and north-west. The Afghans, the wild mountain men, raid them. A handful of English soldiers guard the Indian side of the Pass, like a finger in the hole of the dam.

Metropole Hotel,
Mysore.
(Quarters not so spiffy but very comfortable.)
May 25th.

Darlings,

Saturday afternoon we drove over here to My- *The Road to* sore, ninety miles west from Bangalore. The country *Mysore* changed from the desert red, growing greener and greener and more and more jungly; palm trees, coconut, date and toddy,—seas of them now and again; paddy fields—irrigated; plantations of sugar cane; and great banyan and fig trees all along the road, giving shade; monkeys climbing in them and plopping to the ground.

Now, India did seem populous, a continuous human stream, and Daddy swears there are more cattle than people. The bullocks and buffalo are beautiful and so are the carts. And the goats (for goats) are especially lovely. As for the slender women, in the upward curving line of their saris, balancing lovely *Breath-* things on their heads with delicate arm, elbow, wrist *Taking* and finger upraised in a lovely bow, they are beautiful *Human* —especially when they are carrying two brass pots *Pageantry* one above the other, like a golden temple decoration. Then with their shining pots they group themselves around a well, those women! Oh, there wasn't a sight along that whole road that wouldn't have made a picture and used up rolls and rolls of film. First of all we

passed through the Bangalore bazaar. That alone was
enough to keep one 'shooting' a week.

Mysore Hotel.

Later—in bed.

They think I have malaria, but I think I am going
to fool them. I believe it is nothing but liver again. It
is Gul Kahn who gives me my orders—not to do this,
not to go out, etc. I think he is rather a dear. All his
family were in and about Quetta when the news came
of the terrible earthquake. Daddy, thoughtful as ever,
sent a telegram for him, and when the reply came that
they were all safe, the tears of relief streamed down
his cheeks.

Arabian Nights City   The Indians, official and otherwise, are cordial and
charming. The city is beautiful, park-like, spick and
span, up to date, brilliantly lighted, six palace domes
magnificently flood-lighted. The court, oriental in
colour and pageantry, is conducted on the most ap-
proved English lines. It is all impressively progressive
and Arabian-Nightish at the same time. I can well
believe there is no other state or city in India to com-
pare with it.

Birthday Revels   It is the Maharajah's Birthday Week, and the city is
full and there is a great programme of events every
day—races, polo, animal shows, hunting with the
Mysore hounds, Gymkhana—all in the most heavenly
gorgeous weather, in lovely grounds. And everybody

24　•

[*facing* SRI CHAMUNDESVARI DEVI, TUTELARY
GODDESS OF MYSORE, IN HER CAR

comes from all the plantations and settlements for miles around; guest palaces and jockey and hunt clubs and hotels are all full and overflowing into tents that have sprung up like mushrooms everywhere. Garden parties, teas, a command dinner at Government House, all very much in the English manner with a strong British stamp. Delhi on a smaller scale—all except the Royal Birthday Procession—that was India, an India worth sailing the seven seas to see.

Thousands of the finest horses in regiments of flash- ing colours; be-turbaned troops in gorgeous, exotic livery, astride beautiful mounts caparisoned with leo- pard skins; the royal and sacred elephants, wonderful to see in gold and silver brocade and jewelled trap- pings. And the Maharajah and his heir in the midst of it, in pale green and gold and rose and gold; His High- ness riding upon a pure white Arab charger.

It was no theatrical show but impressive dignity. The Maharajah is a little, pale man with a kind, sad face. His city is his jewel. He goes up every night to his temple and dwelling on his high hill to meditate over it and institute projects for the people—arts and crafts, a silk mill, sandalwood mill, a model farm, a model village, water power—and summons to his projects the best machines, materials and brains of Europe, so that Mysore is the best administered state in India. The personality of the little man, whose essence I feel everywhere, intrigues me mightily.

Daddy met him to-day at the races. Barbie and I sat in the grand stand, part of which is partitioned off for 'H.H.', with a private tea balcony behind. The race-course is a charming place, like everything else carrying His Highness's private stamp, something outwardly English but with an essential difference; a greater charm and delicacy and lightness of gesture.

There is fantasy in it, as there is in the furniture in the Arts and Crafts Institute which we visited, furniture made of the finest native woods after well chosen English models, and then embellished by the loving hand and eye and imagination of India.

We were invited to tea on the balcony. As we sat there, the Maharajah arrived in his carriage and pair, beautifully liveried, driving himself. So presently Daddy was ushered in to meet him and said he had a very pleasant talk, though H.H. didn't distinguish us, apparently, from any other motion picture company.

It is the Dewan, the Prime Minister, whom somebody described as 'a living brain', who has bidden us here. It is the advertisement we shall be to Mysore that he is thinking of. We already have a young reporter from the *Times of India*, writing up everything as we go along.

H.H.'s   The race-horses were beautiful creatures, English,
Stables country-bred, Arab and whalers. H.H. has a stable of three hundred. Barbie and I, visiting the stables, saw every last one of them, and fed the darlings, all craning

their necks out of immaculate stalls to see who's there,
nickering, reaching up for the tufts of sweet green the
syces (grooms) had all tied up in little bunches to give
us. It's a regular show of course. We went the complete round, from the State stallions that have to be a
pure, spotless white and are a breed peculiar to Rajpu-
tana in Central India, through Austrian, English and
Irish beauties to the ponies for the royal children, one of
which, we were told, could beat any horse at racing.

The horses made a fine show, but the bullocks were
really exciting. The most enormous of the bulls, of
some northern breed with a tremendous weight of
horns, lapped up our bouquets of juicy green, as
gentle as a lamb.

The Mysore bullocks are not as patient and long-
suffering as they look. Like elephants, they obey only
their keepers, and are dangerous to all others; also like
elephants they have a long memory and will bear a
grudge. Several keepers tried to make their bullocks
lie down for us, pulling on the rope which passes
through their tender nostrils, but the obstinate beasts
wouldn't. Perhaps H.H. could have made them. He is
evidently one of those who are born with power over
animals.

There are many stories of his power. There was a
bad elephant who had killed three men and wounded
four. He was tied up, waiting for the executioner to
come and end his wickedness with a ball of lead. H.H.

27

came along, walked up to the elephant, said: 'You have been bad but I forgive you this time. Do not do it again.' And from that day to this, that elephant has been good. Again, there was a dangerous dog, so vicious that he was put into a cage like a wild beast and kept there month after month. Said H.H.: 'What have you there? Is that a tiger that you keep him caged?' He spoke to the dog. 'Be good.' And they let the dog out and the dog licked his hand. Believe it or not!

H.H.'s Zoo Anyway, H.H.'s Zoo gives you an entirely different feeling about the animals from any other Zoo that I have ever been in. There are four enormous and most splendid and fearsome tigers. Perhaps it is just because they are so jungly fierce and seem to have lost nothing of their real selves that the Zoo feels like a place where you can meet the animals on their own level. They haven't been shamed or cowed by captivity one little bit. All dignity preserved. That's why it's nice.

After the races we drove up to the top of the hill overlooking the city. H.H. loves this hill, and crowning the tip-top of it he has a house for himself, where he can go every evening to watch his city shining with lights like jewels vying with the stars. We drove like the wind to the top and turning, drove down again, to meet H.H. coming up. This was my first glimpse of him face to face. I forgot my manners. I simply stared.

[facing THE BULLOCKS OF MYSORE ARE A
FAMOUS BREED

His Highness has issued orders to give us all the assistance we need. We may have his elephants. So everything looks rosy.

'Reverend Sir,

In the daily newspaper I just now read the statement regarding your desire to have Kipling's *Toomai of the Elephants* immortalized in the celluloid. May I request your honour to give me a chance of taking however a small part in your ambitious project? Your honour will ask at once "What is your qualification and experience in this line?"

Nothing of the sort, sir, except my sincerity, common intelligence and inquisitiveness, enterprise and intense zeal toward it.

As regards myself, I am a youth of twenty, am five feet nine inches in height. For two years I am studying books on Cinematograph at home, theoretically, but Sir, none has yet extended me any opportunity to try my ability in the practical field to begin my life anew therewith. So at least I seek your favour and shelter.'

'Sir,

I beg to remind you that according to your letter of the 17th May, 1935, I have not received any letter as yet as to what you have decided. Oh Sir, am I doomed? Often I curse the long past day when this idea of acting in film first struck to me and rooted

29

itself in my heart for which I have no means to be freed but to seek your shelter. Can this great ambition of mine not be realised?'

'Respected Sir,

I understand that you are in search of a Mahout boy and you think that he is somewhere in India. Who knows that I am not that boy. I am sending my photograph with this letter. Please see it and let me know if I am the boy of your Dream. I wish I am.'

'Dear Sir,

I am a young lad of eighteen years only but I look very much younger and tender in age. I am very handsome and my complexion is brown-yellow. I keep every information of the world not to speak of screen and stage. I have studied all films minutely that has been shown in India. I can read, write and understand English language very well. This letter will prove my abilities and my command and capacity over the language. It will be no exaggeration if I say I am intelligent and smart. I may be lacking in the techniques and arts of fine actors but I think it is not difficult to develop them under your fatherly care and guidance.'

'To The Manager,

    The Cinema Factory,

       London Film Corporation, Ltd.,

          Mysore.

Sir,

    May I request you to be good enough to let me know if you can take me on your staff on at least Rs. 100 per mensem as an Assistant Manager or Superintendent.

    I am a retired Police Superintendent. I am a motorist and I maintain my own car. I was an actor during my college days in Madras. I can manage your correspondence and put your actors in the way, as I have an eye for art.

    I was acting principal of a Girls' High School before I got into Government Service. I was a private Coach for European and Indian girls appearing for Cambridge and Intermediate Examinations. This is to hint that I know how to keep girl actors in discipline.'

    This, my dears, was Daddy's fan mail, a sample of it, in Bombay. The papers announced that we had come to film Kipling's *Toomai of the Elephants*.

    India is a film producing country. Daddy says it is *Indian Film* the second largest consumer of raw film in the world. *Production* There are over 180 companies in all, small though they may be, that are producing films for their own

31

people in India—films that the western world never sees and that it knows nothing about.

Bombay alone has 19 studios. I don't know how many picture houses it has, but David says they are always packed. The films are hours and hours long, most of them the stories acted out of the old Hindu legends—god and heroes, their loves and difficulties and wonders performed. Of our films they like horror and mystery and westerns, and they *mob* the Tarzan pictures!

We haven't found our 'Toomai' yet. We have been through the Palace elephant stables where the mahouts tend H.H.'s processional elephants, and through the elephant camps where they keep the work elephants—looking for a young mahout son. Now David has gone further afield to the elephant camps in Coorg, Cochin and Malabar—hundreds of miles.

Meantime we are all keeping our eyes open here. Yesterday I spied a likely lad in the hotel yard and hauled him up for inspection. No! He was a 'sweeper' (low caste) and kneeled and kissed our feet. But the little shock-headed urchins who run the roads, herding skittish goats and lumpish buffalos, are good material.

32

[*facing* SHALL HE BE TOOMAI?]

Darlings,

It is the beginning of the monsoon. It is raining now, the first break in the long, long dry season. And it has been late this year in coming and the heat has been more awful this year than for years before. The papers are full of it. So everybody is glad.

We have found our house. Daddy calls the film a *Our Palace* 'natural'—the way we found the house with great elephant heads carved on the entrance gate; a young palace, all for the asking, ideally situated on the outskirts of the town with free vistas of open country, spreading shade-trees full of monkeys, cheetahs prowling at night, derelict wells, and 'quarters' probably full of snakes. Moreover, it is an old, blood-drenched battle-ground where Tipu Sultan, that most lurid usurper of the Mysore throne, fought the English. They say the cries, tramp and tumult of battle still sound at dead of night. With the English was the young Lieutenant Wellesley, afterwards Duke of Wellington.

Daddy and I went to see it to-day. It was all shut up when we got there, with a guard in uniform, a soldier, very formal and rather suspicious of us, in charge. Daddy wouldn't take a step inside until all the doors and shutters were wide opened. 'Fraid of snakes. I must say it hasn't the air of inviting anybody in. It's a bit forbidding; massive, square, high-ceilinged, tile and plaster, about as human as a stone statue and as mysterious. It was built for the Maharajah's grandmother ninety odd years ago. A fortune teller in Paris once told me I should be 'equally at home in a hut or in a palace'. I suppose this is the palace. Daddy says we must have snake charmers come in and clear the place of snakes before we settle in.

We had to find one white character for our story, a white hunter of elephants, 'Peterson Sahib'. There was no mistaking him when we found him, almost at once, in the person of an up-state coffee planter, with a kind and competent, weather-bitten face, most photographable. He, Captain Fremlin, was actually a hunter —a shikari as they call them in India—and a very fine one, the best in Mysore; and a very fine shot, which was to prove more useful than we knew. He had been forty years in the country and could tell us all we didn't know about it. And best of all he played bridge. Now I could keep Daddy off that horrible, exasperating game of Caram!

Next we had to find our locations, i.e. to explore our surroundings for their picturable possibilities and decide where we were going to make our scenes.

Tuesday, June 4th.

Dear Ones,

Two lovely drives yesterday and to-day, looking for jungle locations. Yesterday to the Nilgri (blue)

Hills. The Nilgri Hills gave grand vantages overlook- ing a vast spread of wooded country, dipping and rising in valleys and ridges to a far background of misty blue ranges. Very fine but looked just like Michigan or Vermont, and just as tame; a busy high-road running through it, rattling with motor buses full of people, and plantations of tea and coffee all along the way. And yet this was really truly jungle and not only that, it was *elephant* jungle. A step off the road and you stepped into it.

The first thing that ran across the road was a jackal, then a wild boar, a small, black fellow, then a beauti-ful slender, vivid green snake—the driver said it was not poisonous but would 'spit in your eye'—next a mongoose. Besides the little red-faced, common 'Irish' monkeys, there were trees full of langoors, long-tailed, bushy grey monkeys, and one tree full of less common monkeys that are jet black. We stopped and left word for the jungle men to catch some for us and bring them to the bungalow. The jungle men are naked 'aborigines' with mops of shaggy black hair. They look very likeable. Captain Fremlin swears by them. If you want any animal ask the jungle men.

We went off the road to a dak (traveller's) bun-galow where the keeper says a tiger passes almost every night on his way to his hunting. Coming down in the car we stopped to watch some langoors, and R. and Mrs. Borrodaile caught sight of a snake. It was only a glimpse, but from their description the driver said it was a King Cobra, something that Captain Fremlin in all his forty-two years of jungle life has never seen.

King Cobra We threw stones at the place where we had seen it. The driver was frightened for fear the snake would charge us, as King Cobras and *only* King Cobras do. He was afraid, too, to bring us back along the highway after dark, for then the wild elephants come out on the road, and it is dangerous. One herd, dilly-dallying on this same road, held up traffic for three days, only a little while ago. But to look at the road you never would have believed it, for the jungle is scrub and looks hardly different from a back-yard wood-lot.

Bamboo Jungle It was not until to-day, when we went in another direction to the Kakankote jungle, that I began to realize I really was in elephant country. I watched for the milestones to change to black. All the milestones, elsewhere shining white, in elephant country are painted black, because elephants hate white and will root the white stones up.

The stones turned black when we came past stands of teak forest (the road was lined with processions of bullock carts swaying along with great square logs of teak, iron-heavy, swung under them) into creaking bamboo thicket. That creaking thicket somehow seemed much more jungly than yesterday's forest.

36

[*facing* ROAD TO MYSORE

With its queer creaking, its perpetual 'talking', the
bamboo forest is strange and mysterious, both alluring
and foreboding—just right for elephants. When the
forest fires come the hollow stems of bamboo explode
and crack like rifles; and the sound of it burning is like
the sound of battle.

On the way back we saw the elephants that are kept
for the teak work. They were having their evening
bath and scrub in the river, throwing water over
themselves and rolling in the water on their sides and
grunting and rumbling with content. There were
eleven of them, several good big tuskers and one big
cow, with a dear, kind eye, who was only one year
out of the jungle, but so gentle that we could pat her
trunk, and I loved her on the spot. I can't get over
either the strangeness or the complete lovableness of
these creatures. Their mahouts are a people apart.

The jungle with the little, black, happy skin-and-
bone jungle men in it is a world apart. And from Mysore here you can step into it by merely driving forty
miles, two hours in a car. You watch the mileposts
and, as I say, when they turn coal black with staring
white numbers you are in it. The mahouts made the
big tuskers salute us as we went past.

The sunset as we came back was so beautiful that
everyone is talking about it. The country is wonder-
fully beautiful with extraordinary variety. And the
variety among the people, the number of different

types, is never-ending and fascinating. I long to 'shoot' them all, make a real study of the land and the people, the common every-day life, the Maharajah and his industries, everything—a complete cross-section of a native state. Barbie has been cataloguing her photos up to date; a *brave* show, but still just a beginning.

We now moved into our palace, our 'mahal' Chittaranjan Mahal (Chittaranjan was its family name), and made ourselves at home—ourselves and other creatures besides. . . .

Chittaranjan Mahal, Mysore.
June 28th.

Darlings,

     Things are beginning to happen, thick and fast, *Cobras in* First of all, cobras. The yard is full of them. The first *our Palace* one was caught just at our door step. Last night the watchman found another. The two caught were young ones, so evidently there's a family of them. The bite of the young ones is as deadly as that of the old ones. The little krait, not much bigger than a pencil, can kill in 5 minutes' time. A cobra in a bus in Madras—Madras, the fourth largest city in India—bit first the driver, then three passengers one after another, and all four died, so potent is cobra venom. I can tell you we watch our step! No one has lived in this palace of ours for so long that the creatures have been undisturbed for years.

This morning there was a shout of 'Cobra!' from the yard, but it turned out to be only a tree snake, a thin, speedy, vivid green thread of a thing, with an arrow-pointed head. Again there was a shout from the laboratory side and there was a whopping big scorpion just caught in the goods shed. Great menagerie we have!

On top of this the big palace elephant, Irawatha, *Irawatha* came towering in through our elephant gates to pay *the Palace* us a visit. He is the biggest elephant in Mysore (nine *Elephant* feet eight inches). I love the big fellow. I had a ride, clambered up over his tail-end and sat on a pad, hanging for dear life on to the pad ropes. It was nice on top; easy gait. We went out on to the road and collected some huge branches for fodder and came marching in again. I haven't had such a thrill since I was 'so high'. I do love the old beasts. They are too wonderful. I gave him a loaf of bread, about as big as a crumb to him, and he rumbled in his throat to say 'thank you'.

Chittaranjan Mahal.
(Called now, after us, 'Elephant House'.)
July 4th.

This morning early the yard was full of strange *Snake* pipings, and looking out of the window I saw five *Charmers*

Snake figures spreading out over the dirt plain behind us,
Charmers where derelict ant hills, riddled with holes, denote the
abode of the cobras, of which we have already killed
two on our doorstep. So far no good. They have
piped and played in vain. We wait for the noon-
day sun to add its potency to the charm. Meanwhile
out of an innocent-looking basket are pulled a half
dozen captive cobras to dance for us, their wicked
hoods outspread. They dance and then with a 'swush'
they give a wicked lunge and strike, are picked
up by the tail or anywhere, and gladly of themselves slide back under the dark cover of the basket
again.

The charmers say the snakes are hibernating during
the monsoon, far, far underground, so far they can't
hear the pipings. So they probably won't come out
any more anyway, until it gets hot again.

Menagerie We have scorpions, too; two whopping ones,
picked out of the lab., and a tribe of monks, perfect
pests; lots of fun. Can't leave windows open at night
or they are all through the house, and anyway their
funny faces are always peering in at the windows,
squatting, hopping on the sills, finally all retreating to
the big trees out back, where they attend to their
own affairs with swinging and shrieking.

A man brought two tiny, tiny civet cat kittens.
They don't mew, but cry like birds. Our menagerie is
growing so fast that we have transferred it to a special

40

[*facing* THE CATCH—A 'JUNGLEMAN.'
A SLENDER LORIS, A KIND OF LEMUR

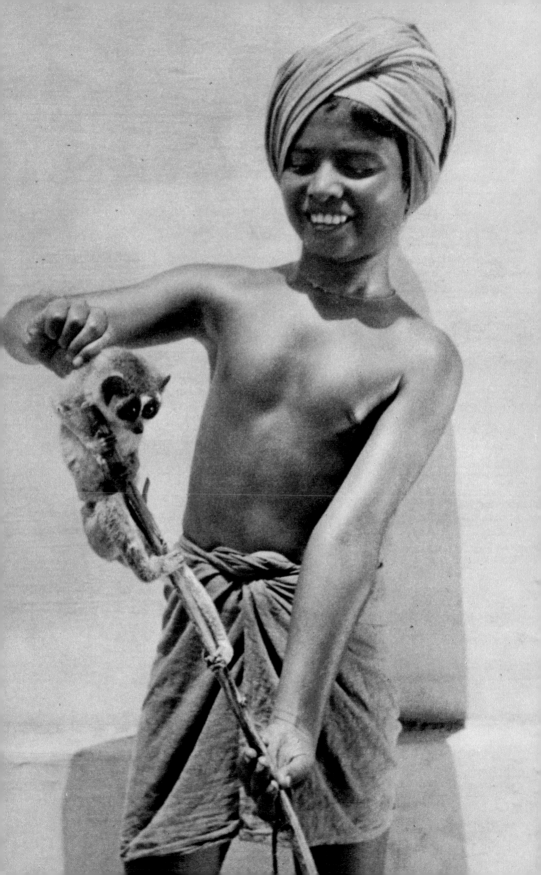

department on the roof, with an animal man, Toni, in charge.

But Toni doesn't have much luck. The four little pups were getting on so beautifully, so fat and roly-poly, and the pie bitch is really a darling mother to them. This morning Toni showed me one of them all shivery and foaming at the mouth. It had rabies. A mad dog had come into the compound and bitten it, bitten its little tongue.

Now we have a baby black buck, and I *do* hope it will live. The mouse deer is still very shy. The baby panther is getting rather rough for play. He squalls up on the roof, squeezed half way through the railings, peering down at us, begging for someone to come up and get him so that he can prowl around the house and chew things up. Daddy's slippers are particularly growly things to chew.

We have been 'shooting'[1] monkeys all morning— our own tribe of monkeys in the trees in our back yard. A wandering tribe of snake charmers and jugglers came around and the minute the python came out of the basket you should have heard those monkeys, the din they made, and how they made a rush through the trees and all hung, fascinated, hair on end, over the basket. Now they have discovered a new game. They are shooting the shoots down the fly

---

[1]'Shooting' with us, of course, never has anything to do with a gun—only the camera.

41

Menagerie of our big tent, swinging up the guy ropes and balancing on the cross pole, a whole row of them with their tails flying S shapes.

The Baby Monkey   Toni caught a baby monkey. I confess we wanted it with a view, of course, to film shots. We nursed it in our spare room; fed it off the fat of the land. It ate, but it cried and cried, pitifully, screwing up its little mouth with such a world of melancholy in its pathetic little eyes. And the unhappy mother hovered about the house, peering in at the baby through the window, moaning. When all the other monkeys had left, she still stayed in the yard, jumping from tree to tree.

At last I couldn't stand it any longer. I took the baby on to the roof. The minute the monkeys saw it, what a bedlam of shrieking and a chatter broke out! I thought I should be mobbed. The mother came leaping to the nearest tree. The baby saw her and began to shriek and struggled in my arms. I slipped the leash. One leap and it was at the edge of the roof, one more and it was in the tree, one more and, oh, my soul, in its terrible fright and trembling hurry it had jumped short.

I saw it hurtling through the branches, and closed my eyes. I heard it strike the ground. I was a murderer, no better. No, thank goodness, the little thing was up and running for dear life, straight into the wide open door of the laboratory. I called out. The whole staff turned to, and the laboratory was searched. A few minutes later out came Ranga Rao, holding at arm's length a small thing dripping wet. The luckless little creature had jumped straight into a tub of water. Yes, it got back to its mother. No more baby catching for us. I thought the monkeys would hate us and desert the compound. But they didn't. Next day they were all back, swinging and shrieking in the trees again; even the baby.

But the other day in the road a monkey was dead. None of our men would touch it. Instead they went to fetch a priest and rose water and incense, in order to perform a proper ceremony to bury it. Yes, the monkey is sacred.

We fixed up a splendid laboratory in the old servants' quarters of our palace—an ideal place for it.

My husband usually travels light on his expeditions, with as little extra work, as few people and as little outfit as possible. It is easier that way, less distracting. There are not so many people and things to keep going then, if one might wish to stop, once in a while, to think.

But this Indian film was different. There was to be no stint of people and everything possible to help us make the picture and make it quickly; which was all very good fun for our large Indian staff; for our confrères from London as well, who were enjoying the whole thing with us.

43

The Outfit I wish you could see us here; you who saw us in Aran! How you would open your eyes! It is so different that we hardly know what to do about it—so many people about, doing for us all the things we have usually had to do ourselves—a fleet of cars flying here and there, a lorry as full of people as a Sunday School picnic plying daily from town (two miles) to our 'bungalow'; thousands of cameras; thousands of racks bursting, bristling with tripods; a stills department with two assistants and I don't know how many still cameras; thousands of carpenters, electricians, tailors, bearers, coolies, sweepers, mahouts, animal trainers, clerks, accountants, interpreters—you would think we were a b . . . . y factory!

We celebrate *'Puja'* We have just had a 'puja'. It comes on a certain day. Everything, all our tools, everything we use, all the various instruments in the laboratory, the weird and wonderful machine which prints film, the huge drum which drives it, and the projector which projects it, all must be worshipped and bowed down to; even the kitchen stove and all the saucepans; and our own selves, sitting on a chair with flower wreaths round our heads and around our necks, and a tinsel-wound flower bunch in our hands and a plate with nuts and raisins and fruit at our feet. We have had it all day. The excitement has been intense and we are all quite

44

[*facing* DHOBIS

Photograph by Barbara Flaherty van Ingen

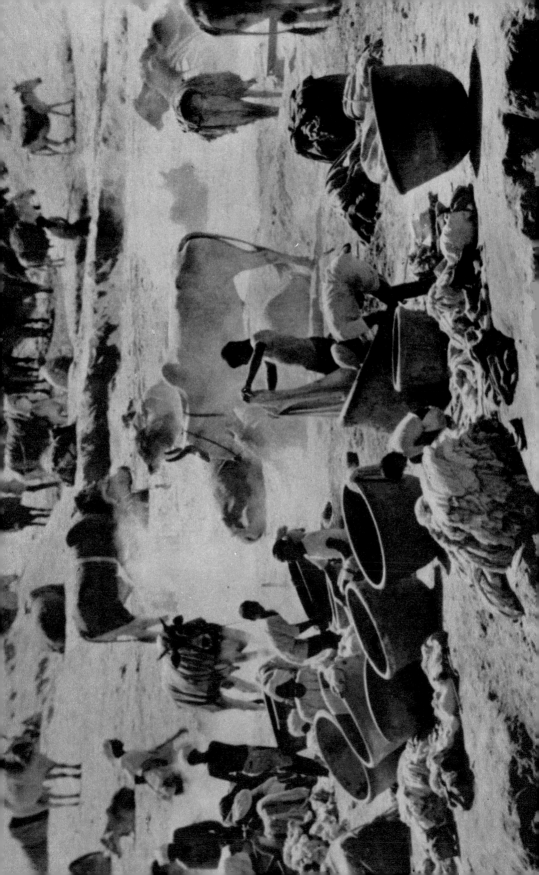

carried away by it. Probably the greatest excitement *We celebrate*
was at the machine shop where a brand new, shining *'Puja'*
circular saw made a particularly splendid thing to
bow to.

But the happiest man of them all was the dhobi. I
had told him he must boil our washing. I upset the
whole tradition of washing which had come down in
his family and caste for generations. It needed a very
extra 'puja'. The new wash boiler was quite hidden
under a mass of flowers and heaped with fruit and
corn and live chickens and other things to eat. Himself, cross-legged, sat earnestly in the midst of it.

It is my sincere sentiment that this custom is a very
fine one. I wish we had it ourselves. The Maharajah
performs it, too. He performs it in public with great
ceremony, worshipping his elephants and horses and
carriages and everything that is his.

We've got a little elephant boy David picked up *Candidates*
somewhere over in Malabar. He is the most endearing *for Toomai*
kid you ever saw. He is supposed to play around the
yard, but no, he much prefers hanging around where
Daddy is and David, whom he adores, and with me.
He is as bright as a dollar: learning something every
minute; learning to repeat his part.

Yesterday morning he came trotting in, eyes spark-
ling, with a letter he had written to 'his manager'. This
morning it was pictures he had drawn with some
crayons David had bought him. And all morning

long he sat on the floor, drawing elephants. He isn't a
real mahout boy, but he isn't a bit afraid. He climbed
right up on a big elephant when even the mahout's
son didn't want to.

We have three others besides, that we have gathered
from here and there all over the country to try out
for Toomai. They are adorable youngsters, but every
one of them too thin. The little mahout boy from the
Palace said he wasn't going 'home for lunch'. He'd
had his meal, his one daily meal, he wasn't hungry.
We sat him down at the table, and he ate like a horse.
I watch them playing around, kicking a football,
shouting and fighting like kids everywhere, and think
of the strange stroke of fate that is hanging over one
of them.

There is one boy among them whom Bordie (Mr.
Borrodaile, our chief camera man) brought in the
other day; found him at the elephant stables. He is
different from the other sprightly little sprouts. He is
rather pathetic, more reserved, an orphan. His mother's family came from Assam, where the people are
part Mongolian. His name is Sabu.

We were now to see some real Indian jungle life.
We were invited to Karapur to take part in an elephant shoot. Karapur is one of the Maharajah's hunting preserves, where he has a hunting lodge and guest
house. We had practically decided on this preserve as

the best location for our jungle scenes. It was to Karapur that we intended to come for them after the monsoon was over. I dreaded the shooting part of this ex-
pedition but we had to have experience and get
acquainted with our jungle and wild actors, and with
the jungle men, and with the forest rangers with
whom we should have much to do.

The game preserve officer was out to shoot five
elephants that had been giving trouble in the teak
plantations near Begur across the river. These were
not rogues, but single tuskers, wild, grown fond of
teak saplings and paddy, and grown bold by succes-
sive raiding of the tempting paddy fields. The natives
are not allowed to carry fire-arms. Tom-toms and
bamboo clackers, Mr. Wild Elephant soon knows,
only make a noise. So the D.F.O. (District Forest
Officer) and the G.P.O. (Game Preserve Officer) get
together and the G.P.O. brings out his big elephant
gun and a company of soldiers.

If you shoot an elephant you must shoot to kill,
both for the poor beast's sake and your own. There
are two places where a well-placed shot is fatal. One
is on the side in the earhole, the other in front at the
top of the trunk. If wounded, the elephant charges,
covering this vulnerable spot by curling up his trunk.

Begur lies across the river from Karapur. One
crosses the river on a bamboo raft. Unfortunately, by
the time we arrived in Karapur the river, swollen by

47

We go out nine days of steady monsoon rain, was so swift and
to shoot high we could not cross. There was nothing to be
Elephants done about it. We spent that day in camp. As a matter
of fact, we spent three days in camp.

Mysore.

Darlings,

Just back from the jungle. Bearer unpacking my
things, fixing up my nice bed, drawing my hot bath.
My! Won't I be the spoiled baby! He is a dear. I love
him like my shadow.

★　　★　　★

Karapur Karapur Camp consists of two bungalows, more
Camp like country houses; one for H.H., the other for
guests. We had the guest bungalow; three suites of
three rooms each—bed, dressing and bathroom. Comfortable, you can imagine. The walls were hung with
framed photographs, which were most interesting, of
former hunting parties. There was H.R.H. the Prince
of Wales, sitting for his picture, the Russian Arch-
dukes eating their breakfasts—this photograph was
dated 1891—and Lord Willingdon holding up a river
catch, a huge mahseer. The bungalow is called Viceroy Lodge.

Viceroy The suites opened on to the verandah, looking out
Lodge on a formal garden of clipped hedges, trimmed yews
and bougainvillea, exotic palms and ornamental cac-

48

[*facing* SHOOTING BEGINS

tus, and away over a vast lawn studded with beautiful, shapely shade-trees and strange imported trees. In the back, the lawn sloped gently down to the river. All this!—when what I had imagined was grass huts and the smell of wood smoke from camp fires. There is even a power plant for electric lighting. So do civilization and wild beasts exist cheek by jowl here in India. It is one of the eternally astonishing things about the country.

Little Sabu had come with us, a little mahout boy we picked up at the Maharajah's elephant stables, who has been gradually eclipsing three other boys for the part of Toomai. He was so thrilled to be the one chosen to come with us, while the other three clung about the car, crestfallen. Arrived at the camp he set at once to work, helping David with the lamps, helping the bearers with the beds, turning the sheets neatly and smoothing them, so busy and happy showing us what he could do.

'Aren't you afraid to come with us?' Bordie had asked him.

'No,' said he, 'I am not afraid of anything in the world. I am here to serve the masters.'

And when we fussed with him over his costume, pulled him and poked him, tucked up his dhoti and wound and re-wound his puggeree (making him look worse and worse, I must confess), he took charge of the matter himself and told *us* what *he* wanted.

D 49

Sabu has his first Film Test He came out finally before the camera and all of us, as we stood around staring, perfectly business-like, self-contained, serious, not a child at all. Perhaps it is because he is an orphan.

That evening there was a bustle and a stir about the other, the Maharajah's, bungalow. Two cars drove up, obviously palace cars, and a truck. Someone of the royal family had arrived. It was Prince Jaya, the Maharajah's nephew and heir.

Our First Shikar as Guests of Prince Jaya Nil Canterau, the G.P.O., came over after dinner to say that he was taking Prince Jaya on a hunt in the morning. Would we accompany the party? What were they going to hunt? Oh, cheetal, sambhur, bison, anything—a trophy for the Prince. He was very keen on shikar. Nil Canterau laughed as he said he would not let him shoot anything but what was big enough to be a worthy trophy for a Prince. We could have for our party one of the hunting elephants with a howdah for four, and would we be ready by five-fifteen in the morning?

So by five-thirty the next morning, as dawn was breaking, we were following the Prince's car down the road. Suddenly four big shadows loomed ahead of us. They were our waiting elephants. With them on foot was a bodyguard with guns from the forest department.

The beauty of hunting with elephants is that you go through the forest as part of the forest. To the wild

50

[*facing* REFRESHMENTS ON THE WAY

creatures by scent and sound you are only one of
them. Animals don't look up as a rule, and anyway
they accept the cow elephant on which you ride as a
wild one. They pay no attention; you go among them
like Mowgli. Ahead of you, of course, go the little
jungle men. They are your eyes and ears, seeing
everything, hearing everything, knowing every sign.
Without them one might wander days and days and
the forest be as empty of life and silent as a tomb.
They tread ahead of you, stepping warily, plant-
ing their feet firmly and cautiously on the jungle
ground.

The elephants follow in single file, the head elephant breaking trail, bending trees out of the way with
his head and breaking them with his foot, reaching
with his trunk to break away the branches overhead.
Slow progress but steady, down deep 'nullahs' (ra-
vines) when the howdah is almost straight up and
down and the elephant places each foot with the utmost care and stretches his hind legs straight out behind to act as a brake, climbing the other side by
doubling up his forelegs at the knees and pushing
himself up, up, encouraged, of course, by the 'hup,
hup' of his mahout.

The nullahs are exciting, for there in the soft mud
or sand will be marks clear enough for the veriest
amateur to read. I saw the pug marks of a tiger,
its five cushions as fresh as paint, and the track of

the bison we were following cut deep and clean as a knife in the dark-red clay.

On the head elephant rode the Prince, Nil Canterau and Colonel Locke; behind us came Daddy, Bordie and Captain Fremlin on a dear old cow with kind, tired eyes and hollow cheeks, like those of an old, old woman. Cows only are safe to use for hunting in elephant country, for the wild male is a chivalrous knight—he will attack the tame tusker but never the cow. Bringing up our rear came a baby elephant, half grown, the cutest thing you ever saw, his load the commissary department, bristling with baskets and bright brass cans.

All of them fed as they came along, their trunks feeling along the path ahead for young bamboo shoots and succulent grasses and curling around them. The grasses came up by the roots and the swishing and slapping of these grasses, as they shook them this way and that to free the roots of soil before they daintily tucked them up into their mouths, was like the slapping of wet sheets blown in the wind. Slap, slap, munch, munch, tramp, tramp, while we on top ducked the overhanging branches or broke them away. So for four hours.

Animals
we see We saw a beautiful squirrel, with a body as big as a badger and a tail like a fox, flying through the branches overhead. Daddy saw a grey, black-faced langoor, with a tail (he swears) six feet long. Bordie

52

[*facing* HEAD TRACKER FOR THE PRINCE'S SHIKAR.
ALMOST BLIND HE TRACKS BY SCENT

saw a mouse-deer. And then we ran into a herd of cheetal, but with no stag among them big enough for a trophy, said the jungle men. On. On. At noon we stopped for lunch. A rug was spread under a tree, and out came the brass cans and what not. Most interesting. There were individual brass cans that were triple deckers, white rice with sour curds in one compartment, yellow rice with vegetables and herbs in another and in the third a hot, peppery combination of victuals that I couldn't tell you what they were. Anyway, it was all exceedingly good.

It is remarkable how grateful those hot things, *Good eating* curry and the like, are to the stomach in these climates. I believe one needs them. Our miserable ham sandwiches looked too disgusting, cold, limp, colourless, tasteless. Ugh! Out of the big brass cans came more white rice and yellow rice in great handfuls for the jungle men. Their staple food is a cheaper but more nutritious grain like wheat, called 'ragi'. The rice was a treat. They sat happily in a circle, the rice piled on leaves before them, royally served by the palace servants, and ate with their fingers.

After lunch we came into different jungle. The trees were heavier, the undergrowth was grass, which in a few more weeks of monsoon would be higher than a man,—ten feet, they say. We were still tracking the bull bison, but most of us, replete with lunch, were lurching along half asleep and not thinking of

53

Tiger! anything. When suddenly there was a signal from the party ahead. 'TIGER!' And the Prince's gun went off with a shattering bang.

We all stood up in our howdahs (the elephants never turned a hair) and some of us saw one tiger, some saw two. I never saw either of them. I didn't know whether the tiger was wounded, whether he was right over there, lurking in the grass ready to spring, or what. The grass all about was lain on and trampled. And just then a huge herd of bison broke cover, but some distance away, too far for a photo. (I always seemed to have the wrong lens on my camera, anyway, worse luck!) Our elephants weren't the least excited by all this. Why not? Were we not in the slightest danger, then, that they might stampede? I asked Nil Canterau about it. He said a tiger had only to rumble out a growl and rap the ground with his tail to make a whole herd of wild elephants stampede. What about ours, then? They were trained hunting elephants. But Nil Canterau laughed his hard, gusty laugh, as he said it was probably just as well the Prince had missed, for we could well imagine what it would be like to be bolted with through that jungle. So I gathered that a wounded tiger is nothing to sneeze at, even with elephants trained to hunt.

Minor Ailments The next day was a wash-out. I had colic and Daddy had a sore foot from walking about these infected floors barefoot. We stayed at home and nursed our-

54

selves on the verandah like two old crows, while the *Minor Ailments* others went hunting with the Prince again. They were to be back early. Mid morning we heard bang, bang, reverberating from their direction. They were surely having sport. Curse the luck. Noon time and they hadn't come back. Three o'clock and still no sign of them. I began to imagine all sorts of things.

Sabu was unhappy too. I heard a sob from the *Sabu has his Troubles* depths of a verandah chair. He had had no sugar in his coffee (our stores happened to be low). The cook had been unkind to him. (Poor cook!) And he ouched and writhed in bitterness of spirit as I applied iodine where an old scab was a little broken. Gone was all his yes-terday's aplomb. Sabu was just a lonely, homesick, heartsick little boy.

At about four-thirty we went out along the road in *Jungle Road* the car. This is the time when everything begins to happen along the road and I love to be out in it. There is the never-ending wonder of the sheer numbers of the droves and droves of cattle, and goats as delicate as deer, with pointed horns and delicate hoofs that patter along the road like rain. They pour out from the jungle where they have been grazing all day. The herd girls and boys, mere children, stare out of big eyes and tousled heads. They dare the jungle and the jungle roads, I suppose, because there are so many of them. The same with the slow procession of the bullock carts, never-ending day and night.

The Company   From end to end of India they trek unceasing. It is
of the Road like a sort of nightmare to think of it. It is like the
migration of ants one sees, no beginning, no end, un-
broken, crowding, jostling, a whole mysterious way
of life beyond all common comprehension. As they
are creaking by, or resting with patient bullocks in the
shade, I must always scan the faces of this vast company of the road. Some are wild and fanatical, some
gentle and fine. The faces of women and children peer
out from the frames of the oval basket-work hoods. I
wonder at the great size and iron weight of the teak
logs they carry and what else there is of cargo to keep
them ever moving, moving. The patient bullocks are
strong. Tipu Sultan with his bullocks had the better of
the English with their horses. He could move forty
miles while they moved twenty.

Jungle   Some five miles beyond Karapur the real jungle
Villages villages begin. They are exquisite. Thatched roofs
nestle in banana groves at the forest edge, where the
forest is cut like a slice, showing black behind the
white boles of enormous trees, or tender green and
fine as gossamer where giant bamboo fronds make a
feathery screen and plume the sky higher than a
palm. Before them gleams a great flat stretch of paddy
fields, like a mirror-mosaic, flooded by the rains,
viridescent where the rice seedlings are just sprouting; beautiful, slender figures of women with shining
brass pots on their heads coming across them, thread-

56

[*facing* '. . . THE CONTINUOUS PROCESSION OF THE
BULLOCK CARTS . . .'

ing the narrow, dyke-like paths. I have never seen anything more beautiful anywhere. I wished I knew the people. They were evidently not the Kuruba jungle folk but quite different, an old people. One girl I couldn't keep my eyes from. Her hair, smoothly oiled and pulled back from her brow, was decorated at the back with a flower wreath; on top of her head she had plastered a green fern, its fronds spread out. And there it stuck. You can't imagine how effective it was.

Groups of men were eating beside their bullock carts. They were most friendly and ready to satisfy my curiosity on every point. They were making a meal off bamboo sprouts, a green berry out of which they were pounding the seeds, and some green leaves. David says that the bamboo shoots, which look so good, are acrid.

Coming home, a pea-hen with her chick crossed the road. A little farther on a gorgeous cock trailed its sweeping tail. We stopped and watched it strutting away quite unconcerned, a glowing spot of colour through the brown stems of bamboo.

The hunters were there, all intact, when we got home. They had stayed out to track an elephant herd. No shooting, but just the wonder that they could come so close. A bison happened to be with the elephants and took alarm. Otherwise they could have mingled with the wild herd, even as Toomai mingled

Film problems with them in the elephant dance. If we could only operate the cameras from elephants' backs in the jungle! We have to get the wild elephants moving through the forest. Our script demands also that we get two tuskers fighting.

The fight can be staged in the mating season in September, says our Jemadar. Wild tuskers will be decoyed into an area trenched around by a four-foot trench, an insuperable obstacle to an elephant, because he cannot span it and cannot jump. The decoys will be tame cows, and that the fight will ensue is, according to everyone, a foregone conclusion. If the tuskers are equally matched it will be a great show. Prince Jaya has already spoken for a front seat!

Monday.

Recruiting the 'Key Man'

The Jemadar

One more day in camp to see the elephants swim the river and to talk with the Jemadar. The Jemadar is the chief of mahouts of the Kakankote camp, the best trainer of elephants in the country. We have had quite a time negotiating for him. He will be an important person for us. We have to depend on him to make the elephant do the things we want, and to teach him a trick or two besides. You remember the Jungle Book picture, where Kala Nag holds Little Toomai up in his trunk? We have seen no elephant and heard of only two who are supposed to be able to do that. But the Jemadar says Lakshmi Prassad, the big tusker of the Kakankote camp, can be taught to do it, though it may take some months. It will be interesting watching how he does it, won't it?

We came upon our old shikar elephants at the river, having a glorious bathe after their two days hunting. They were coming out of the water all clean and black and shining. I loved seeing them again, like old friends. I could imagine they recognized us. We made much of them, patting them. The one I thought so old is not old at all, not full grown, but she had a bad time, poor thing, bearing a calf which was born dead. Her eyes are so patient and so kind. Though only a year and eight months caught, she seems gentlest and wisest of all.

Sabu, transfigured, was in his element, thoroughly at home, ordering the elephants about, mounting them, riding them, sitting there as on a throne from which he looked down upon us common mortals. It is here, by the way, near Kakankote, that he was born. His mother died when he was a baby. His father taught his elephant to rock the baby's cradle—to rock the baby himself in his trunk. It is even said that a wild elephant came out of the forest and played with the child!

The river, as I have said, was mightily swollen by the heavy monsoon rains,—a racing torrent three hundred yards across. Bob was curious to know if the elephants would tackle such a current, and asked the

mahouts if they would care to try it, offering a most
attractive reward. They were all willing but in spite
of their most violent urging, not an elephant would
go beyond his depth and face the stream.

Finally the chief mahout came down, and we asked
him if among all his elephants there was one strong
enough to swim the river. Yes, he had one. It was
Lakshmi Prassad, the Jemadar's big tusker, our pro-
spective star.

Lakshmi forthwith was made ready for the swim.
A rope was put around him, by which the mahout
would be enabled to hold on against the raging current. Sabu, very busy, kneeling on Lakshmi's broad
back, helped strap the rope around him. The mahout
mounted to his seat on Lakshmi's neck. Sabu settled
himself, sitting behind the mahout. He was going
too! I didn't like it. I was afraid. Was it surely all
right?

They launched into the river. The bank was sheer
and almost at once the elephant had lost his footing
and was swimming, swimming strongly, his head up,
and then under, up and under. Mid-stream, the current caught them, a swirling, whirl-pocked flood. The
elephant could make no more headway and began
sliding downstream. He was now completely under;
only the tip of his trunk showing; and Sabu and the
mahout were down to their armpits. We were in a
panic. We had not guessed the river's strength. Twice,

[*facing* MONSOON
Photograph by Barbara Flaherty van Ingen

Sabu told us afterwards, he lost hold of the rope. Just as well we didn't know that as we watched them—his little figure holding on for dear life, the mahout, and the head of the elephant bobbing like a cork as the current bore them down, down.

Below them, fortunately, the river made a wide bend. Here at last they touched bottom and clambered up on shore. We all broke out shouting. Sabu waved. There was no longer any doubt who was to be our elephant boy!

Chittaranjan Mahal.
July 12th.

Darlings,

Oh how this monsoon wind is blowing, and how it blows around this house! Usually it dies down a bit between sunset and sunrise and there is only a faint moaning around the eaves and through the window cracks. But last night there was such a blast I couldn't sleep. With the window shut, my mosquito net slapped and banged like a ship's sail. And I couldn't help thinking of you two, if this wind keeps on, in the Indian Ocean. You would be going up and down, the way I dreamed of seas that mounted so high that I couldn't see their tops above the sky-scrapers and then came down sickeningly, and there was a wee boat going up and down on them. Horrible dream! I am *very* brave to let you come.

Barbie has been breaking in a new assistant for her-
self, and evidently they spend most of their time in
the dark room talking religion, etc. Religion is the
great prepossession here. The first thing our good-
looking young sergeant riding master asked me when
he finally got a personal word with me was what my
religion was. And the topic lasted all the way across
the big maidan. Everything we ask about is explained
to us from the point of view of traditional belief—the
gods, religion, morality, idealism; every tree we ask
about, every flower we notice is connected somehow
with religious belief and custom. It is almost weird. The
strength of it is something quite inconceivable to us.

Brahmins   Looking for a location, one day, we came to a
river. By the banks of the river were two very spiffy
motor cars. We looked down the bank and there out
in the stream, seated like a white-robed Buddha in a
bathing ghat, was he who was evidently the prosper-
ous owner of the cars, and his family, scooping up
portions of filthy river water, pouring it (like a soda-
fountain clerk) from one cup to another, praying and
drinking. Once in every twelve years the water of the
sacred river Ganges is supposed to be diverted into
this river, and this is the year. Along the banks of the
river there was such a stench of excreta that you
couldn't walk there, and just back of the temples was
the foulest drainage ditch I ever did see. Isn't it in-
credible!

[*facing top:* THE BRAHMIN BOY IS TRAINED IN
THE RITUAL OF HIS FAITH TO CARRY ON ITS
SPIRITUAL AND TEMPORAL AUTHORITY
bottom: IN MELKOTE BURNS THE FLAME OF
BRAHMIN PRIESTHOOD

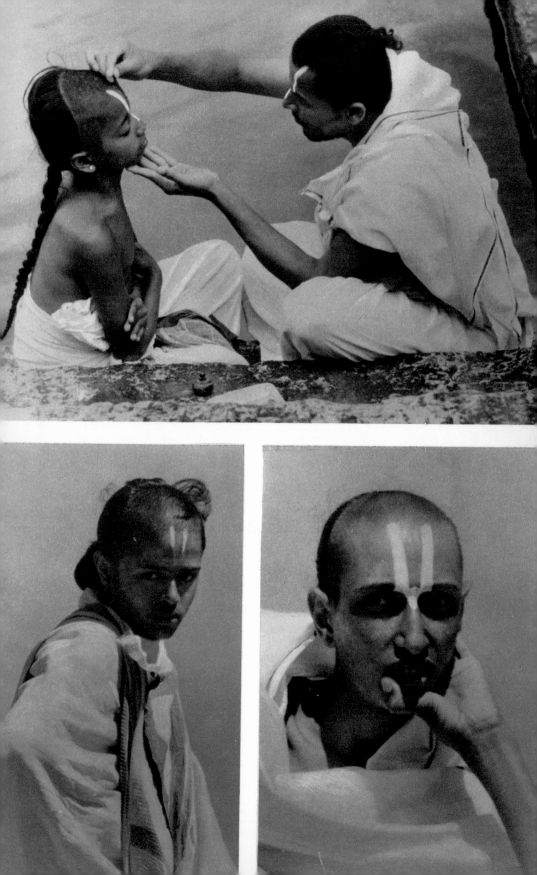

The next day we bumped into a Mohammedan religious festival at the tomb of Haidar Ali and Tipu Sultan, Mohammedan usurpers for a short time (about a hundred and fifty years ago) of the Mysore throne. And now their memory is kept very green indeed by the faithful who worship as a god this bloody man who was nothing but a common sepoy, commonest of the common, but with a flair for generalship, a lesser Napoleon.

I must say that his tomb, all dazzling white with massive ebony-black polished stone pillars, was impressive, dignified and beautiful. His gardens were full of every sort of strange plant and tree, which he had raided from all over India, and they made this day a most enchanting setting for the gay-coloured people; family parties everywhere, the women *for this one day*, so I was told, not veiled, the young girls with round jewelled nose-rings, the babies (if they had not another rag on) with the most elaborate velvet gold-embroidered caps.

The barbaric, elaborate finery of the Mohammedans is a contrast to the greater simplicity of the Hindu. It is the way I distinguish them. The family parties had all come in the usual way, by bullock cart. We parked the car near one that was resting by the roadside. It made a nice picture. Out came the cameras and out popped the family; one, two, three, four, five, six, seven, eight, nine, ten, eleven, *twelve children* all

63

of an age, and the three wives, and the paterfamilias himself. How do they live?

Coming back to town we passed the women who pick grass. A little sparse grass grows along the roadside, cropped to the bare soil by the flocks and flocks of goats and sheep and cows that throng the roads all day and all night. Women go along digging at these stumps of grass, pluck them out by the roots, wash off the soil and sell them in the market.

Barbie and I have been to see the silk mills, and the sandalwood oil mills, two of the boasts of Mysore's *Progressive* modern and progressive administration. They had the *Mysore* best of everything. At the silk mills, dyes from Germany, machinery from France, the famous gold thread of Lyons, made in Bangalore by brothers of the famous family in Lyons who have made this gold thread for generations. And at the head of the spinning department a darling little Japanese woman, *The Silk* who showed and explained everything with so much *Mills* smiling pride. I could only understand half her eager stream of words, but did you know that each small yellow cocoon has wound upon it three hundred to five hundred metres of *one*, fine gossamer thread?

The delicate brown hands of the Indian workers (mostly women) working in this spinning maze of gossamer threads was as wonderful as a dream. They get eight annas (ninepence) per day.

[*facing* SADHUS, BEGGING THEIR WAY FROM SHRINE TO SHRINE. LIVING VESSELS OF PRAYER— EACH CRUMB THEY BEG AN OFFERING TO THE GODS

At the sandalwood mills we learned one thing of particular interest. The oil, besides its use as a scent, is a powerful antiseptic. The jungle people use it for their cuts, and not only the people, but elephants. An elephant will choose a ripe tree and uproot it and peel the bark and rub his sores. Like an iodine pencil!

Also I went to the opening session of a real Hindu wedding, through Barbie's Indian Gentleman Friend. It was his son's wedding. Everybody else thinks the I.G.F. a great bore but I think he is so humorous and pathetic. His every other word is 'etiquette'. He and his wife go to the movies; only the English movies, not the native ones, oh no! Because in the English movies they know that everything they see is 'etiquette' and so they learn. We must be sure to tell him when his etiquette wasn't just right. He embarrassingly presses gifts and more gifts and more invitations upon us, all for Barbara, while she makes caricatures of him as a wangling old humbug, as perhaps he is.

Anyway, the wedding was so pure Indian that it was startling to see our I.G.F. sitting cross-legged upon a canopied dais, beside his son, with a crowd of Brahmin priests squatting about, performing a whole rigmarole of ritual, long-drawn out—the wedding lasts a week—with offerings to the gods spread out— so simple—bits of food, bananas, and flowers, and the dedicated household grinding-stone and other homely

E 65

implements, and behind all these the temple musicians and dancing girls keeping up a continuous droning chant, drumming and fiddling and dancing.

Temple dancing girls sound so romantic. I have always thought of them as the fairest and choicest of their sex. But these were both old and not shapely. They danced with their hands *much* like the Samoans. The sweet, heavy scent of the jasmine flowers was like Samoa. But the bride, besides flowers, had fine jewels and a costly sari woven of gold and rose colour. She was very lovely, demure, eyes downcast. She had been to England more than once and was 'well educated', our I.G.F. repeatedly assured us. But that, most obviously, was going to make little difference to her now that she was about to become a purdah wife.

There were two women there who were thoroughly westernized and emancipated. One little body looked like anything but what she was, Mysore's first woman B.A. The other, with more apparent distinction, was the head of the Maternity Hospital here. Both in saris, for only the half-caste discards this badge of beauty.

The Borrodailes, too, stumbled into a wedding of lower caste and were eagerly pressed to join the guests. The host claimed to be a barrister, but their description of the sanitary horrors they had to witness and even, out of politeness not refuse to *swallow*,

66

was too amazing. Indians love to get B.A.'s and A.B.'s, etc.—educational tags. It gives them a coveted standing and prestige. But they never think of applying what they learn to their daily way of living and doing things, which may be thousands of years old and almost as primitive.

It is the season of weddings. Yesterday we took a long drive to see one of the monumental sights of Mysore, a colossal Jain statue, about sixty to seventy miles from Mysore City. We passed through many villages and stopped to eat in a dak bungalow. This village, like the others we had passed through, was full of pipings, thin, translucent pipings. There were three little groups of people circling in among the houses, each with a band of musicians. Our driver said they were wedding parties. Would they, one of them, come over to the bungalow?

They came readily, the young bridegroom and his bride, shy and solemn, almost expressionless (he was eighteen and she was twelve) led by three musicians playing on a drum and two pipes and a little crowd following behind. After taking pictures I put the silver pieces that Gul Khan gave me into the two cupped hands of the little bride. She folded her hands, put them to her forehead like a temple priestess and bowed.

Then suddenly an old man stepped forward and began to jabber something and his voice broke and tears came to his eyes and I thought he was putting on a begging show to get more money. Not at all. He was only telling us how all his family were dead and this was his last, his only grandchild and wouldn't we please take for him a picture of himself with her. He was a sweet old man and the whole scene was very affecting. I am sure there was a lot of solemn and sweet ritual to the little ceremony that we didn't see. This was only the affiancing. By a recent law she cannot be married until she is sixteen.

We went on until we came to a hill that rested on the plain like a huge boulder. We had to be carried up it, swung on the shoulders of four bearers in a sort of wooden cradle. It was a fearful contraption and I did pity the poor bearers puffing and sweating in the full heat of the hot afternoon. A tiny tot of a boy came along with them and gave them a hand, pushing mightily with cheery 'Hump-hah's'. The bearers put down the cradle every now and then and mopped
their brows and smiled at me.

As you approach the top of the hill you see a great stone head and shoulders against the sky above a temple wall. It is a colossal statue, the biggest stone figure in the world carved out of a single block of granite. Wrought with utmost simplicity, there is yet such a feeling of the texture of flesh about it that you wonder it can be stone. Its date is A.D. 983, and yet it is as fresh and perfect both in conception and execution as

68

[*facing* GOMATA SRAVANA BELGOLA. COLOSSAL JAIN
STATUE, CARVED OUT OF A SINGLE BLOCK
OF GRANITE. A.D. 983

though it had come yesterday from the sculptor's hand. The figure represents a seer who has stood so long in the perfect immobility of profoundest meditation that the ant hills have grown up about his feet and the vines entwined his limbs. Once every while there rises up about the statue a colossal scaffolding. This is for a ceremony—one of the ceremonies of India's cult of fertility. Votaries swarm in every part of the structure and pour milk, human milk and sacred cow's milk, over the figure. The face is unforgettable. I shall always think of it looking out over the wide plain, with the little wedding procession circling a perpetual dance beneath it.

The I.G.F. came again to-night, with his funny black face. Everyone still thinks him a bore, but I like to hear him talk. Bob says his stories aren't true, and makes fun of the way he goggles his eyes and purses his lips as he makes his effects. He told us most affectingly of the Maharajah's illness. We could follow its progress from day to day and hour to hour, through the journey to Bangalore and the next morning's ride. He had shown consideration for everyone, protesting that he was all right, that they must go on and ride, everything must go on as usual, until his legs gave way and they caught him as he fell.

'I feel so queer,' he kept saying, 'I feel so queer. Where is my turban?' (He couldn't feel it on his head.)

'Why did the tailor make my coat without a pocket?' (He couldn't feel his pocket.)

We listened and felt as intensely as though we were hearing about a personal friend.

Now they say he is all right again, is walking and going about and will be back in Mysore soon. Mysore will be like a temple with its divinity restored. I don't know what it would be like without H.H.,—not the same place.

To-day the I.G.F. told us what the Maharajah does every day, and no wonder he is frail. Up at five, Indian exercises, then European ones; then the race-course—four trotting horses waiting, three times round, once galloping, once trotting, then galloping, trotting and walking; then bath, worship, and a weak cup of coffee; then sees his secretaries. Ten to eleven, visits Zoo, stables, garages, band office. Before break-fast, I forgot to say, he drives through a section of the city with a notebook to see if it is clean, etc. The afternoon he begins with music, writes private letters, sees his secretaries again, receives the Resident and other officials. At five-thirty, tennis, then talking, then bath, worship. At nine a cup of milk, then the newspapers, then reading, philosophy, bed.

Do you believe these other stories, also told by the I.G.F.? The first one is about Lakshmi Prassad.

In the Keddah stockade with the wild elephants his mahout slipped off and fell to the ground. A wild tusker was about to trample and tear him. Lakshmi charged the tusker, seized the mahout with his trunk and pushed him to safety between his legs, then watching his chance took hold of him again and lifted him up on to his back. Do you believe it?

A mahout died in the jungle, leaving a motherless child. The elephant took charge, fed the child, getting fruit for it, and rocked its cradle with his trunk, wouldn't let anybody come near.

A new temple elephant came to Mysore with his mahout, who then went away. But no sooner was he gone than the elephant would have nothing to do with his new mahout, but took one smell of him and was going to tear him up. So they had to telegraph for the old mahout to come back and no one could go near the elephant until he came.

And how's this one? A mahout was bad to his elephant, underfed him, stole the rations that he should have given him. One day he gave the elephant a rotten cocoanut. The elephant kept the cocoanut in his cheek. He kept it there a month. Then the Inspector came. As soon as he saw the Inspector, out he spewed the bad cocoanut in front of him, then seized his mahout and threw him after the cocoanut.

But what is perfectly true is that elephants, left to graze in the forest, will come charging when they hear the call of the mahout, running to him like a dog. This happens in Assam.

The Elephants We had had such marvellous glimpses of all sorts of animals on our shikar with the Prince that we now began to think how we were going to get a film of them. One obvious way was to set up our cameras somewhere and drive the animals past them. It sounded simple and exciting. Thus my husband, writing to the 'Home Office'—the Studio in London:

'Though the weather was almost impossible for good camera work, I arranged with Captain Fremlin to make a drive for us through a certain portion of the Bandipur preserve. He recruited some hundred and fifty jungle men and located for our three cameras a natural clearing in the jungle. Here at three strategic points the jungle men made blinds for us of branches, and we set up our cameras. Then Fremlin went off with his hundred and fifty jungle men to a distance of about two miles and began his beat toward us.

A Trial Drive 'To me it was more of a try-out than anything else, and I was curious to see just what the technique of the beat was and learn something of it for the big drives which we would stage when the good weather came, after the monsoon. We didn't expect to see anything more formidable than a few herds of deer, possibly some bison, some wild pig and maybe a leopard.

'After Fremlin had gone off, the Game Preserve Officer, who was with us, confided to me that some two months previously they had pulled off a similar drive and expecting nothing more than a few deer

72

[*facing* IRAWATHA'S TRAINING

and other small game took with them only some light
rifles. That particular drive netted a rogue elephant
from which, however, all of them succeeded in escaping but this officer's assistant. Instead of running he
climbed a tree. Unfortunately the rogue saw him,
uprooted the tree and killed him. As we all stood there
behind our cameras waiting for the drive to come on,
I think everyone of us wondered if the drive would
net another rogue elephant.'

So did I, for, as I wrote to the children:

It was Captain Fremlin, Barbie and myself, with
the beaters who were doing the beating. And we
knew the preserve was full of things. We had seen
lots of cheetal, had seen a special place where a tiger
is fed every night upon a buffalo tied out for him, and
we had tracked a bull bison until we had come upon
a large herd.

Now we were going to drive through the jungle in
a wide arc. The beaters spread out according to plan.
Captain Fremlin shot off the rifle and brought down a
crow—lucky sign—which was the signal to advance,
and slowly, slowly we began to beat. It was lovely
fun. Step by step, softly so as not to make a crackle,
then stop, look, listen, no talking above a whisper. On
again, step by step. There was a delicious cool, wet
breeze blowing and not a mosquito; lots of birds and
peacocks calling on all sides. They mew like a cat.

But not a twig snapped, not a grass stirred, not a creature of any kind did we see, not even a deer, all the way up to the cameras, where Daddy's red face peering out of his hide-out, like a Jack-in-the-box, was as frightening as anything!

The poor Captain was a crestfallen man. He suspected that jungle dogs had been hunting through the preserve and cleared everything out. That afternoon we had proof of it. A beautiful sambhur hind came leaping out on to the road in front of the bungalow. Pie dogs were chasing it, leaping at its throat, on its flanks, trying to hamstring it. We chased the dogs off and the poor thing staggered to the ground where it lay, making pitiful sounds, struggling, but too exhausted to get on its feet again. Jungle dogs had chased it as far as the road and then the village dogs had caught on. We kept the dogs off and sent to fetch water for it, but by that time it was on its feet and staggering off into the jungle again.

When we came back to the bungalow late this afternoon, Irawatha, the elephant, was having his lesson. He and Sabu were rehearsing Scene One. Everyone was laughing delightedly to see them. The big elephant was stealing the sugar cane out of Sabu's hand, raising his foot to be punished and squeaking, all to order. Sabu, his little brown body in nothing but a tight-fitting breech cloth, was a perfect thing of beauty.

74

I sometimes have an uncanny feeling about Sabu. *Coincidence*
This is the boy we *imagined* way back in '29 when we *or Predestina-*
were writing our story in Germany. We wrote down *tion?*
in so many words:

'He is a little orphan boy and hanger-on of the
Maharajah's stables.'

And then we wrote:

'His father died, and the elephant, the beloved elephant who had been in the family since his grand-
father's time, went mad with grief and broke his
chains and went off into the jungle.'

And now here is Sabu in the flesh, a little orphan
Indian boy, ward of His Highness's stables. And they
have been telling us the story, how when his father
died his elephant grieved so that no one could do anything with him and there was nothing to do but take
him to the jungle where he ran away—our imagined
story and Sabu's true story almost identical. It was as
we were writing our story that all this happened to
Sabu, six years ago.

It was already October. Five months of our allotted
year were gone and so far we had done little system-
atic shooting, as there had been no weather for it.
But now the monsoon showed signs of breaking.
Everybody said we might begin to count on clear
weather, so we made ready to stage the opening
scenes in our script.

75

These scenes called for a village setting, and for this location we had chosen the most picturesque village we could find anywhere not too far from Mysore. For we had to take all our elephants there, and elephants travel at the stately processional rate of ten miles a day, and have to be provided with cartloads of fodder—green branches—on the way.

I pity the trees in India. Their shapes are grotesque, and this is because they are chopped and lopped from the time they have a branch or a leaf to spare, to make food for the goats. The damage is done with long rake-handled, hook-shaped knives. Our way to Melkote, I thought, with elephant appetites eight hundred pounds per day per head, was going to be a Golgotha for the poor trees. But that is beside the point.

Melkote Travellers' Bungalow.

Darling Mon,

Here we are in camp, with all the tents, two grass huts and twelve elephants. There should have been fourteen elephants but two of them had to be left half way, under painful circumstances. We had just been filming the whole long file of them coming alone through a lovely screen of banyan strings, with the twin minarets of Seringapatam dazzling white behind them.

Elephants, cars, trucks, cameras and crowds of

[*facing* WEAVERS OF MELKOTE

villagers with their carts and bullocks and flocks were all bunched together when Irawatha suddenly took a dislike to the tusker next to him, let out a roar and gave him an awful push and dig with his tusks. The poor tusker squealed and gave a great bound. His mahout came tumbling off and rolled in the dust, his eyes fairly bursting out of his head. Everybody scrambled and scattered. The other elephants rapped their trunks angrily on the ground, ready for a fray. Little Sabu, perched all alone on Irawatha, was whacking away at his head with the goad, his arm going up and down and up and down like a sledge hammer.

It was all over in less time than it takes to tell. The poor tusker, down behind and up at the head, had his tusks jammed in the thatch roofing of a house so that he couldn't move. Irawatha would have finished him, but just then the Jemadar stepped in, suddenly appeared between them. Facing Irawatha he put a hand on each great tusk. It was an astonishing sight,— Irawatha mad, with already a taste of blood, his great head lowered and behind it his great bulk gathered for a final charge, and the Jemadar, with not enough of him even to fill his clothes, and nothing but a little stick in his hand—a little cane as thick as a match-stick he always carries with him and with which he sometimes raps Irawatha's trunk—pushing Irawatha back!

Irawatha had to have a long, heavy chain put on from his neck to his forefoot. His mahout rode with a hatchet raised ready over his head, and the Jemadar walked beside him, carrying a long, steel-pointed spear. When, for the picture, we had to put Sabu on him alone, a mahout lay concealed under the pack-cloth behind Sabu, ready to pop out in case of trouble.

Yesterday, a white spot appeared on Irawatha's temple between his eye and his ear where there is a little hole in his head. From this hole, fluid oozes out when an elephant goes 'musth', and 'musth' is a sickness elephants have, during which they go mad.

To-day we learned that Irawatha is 'musth', which means that we cannot work with him until he is well again, and nobody knows how long that may be—three weeks or three months. So now we have to begin to train in another big tusker, Lakshmi Prassad, four inches shorter than Irawatha, very clever, but rather bad, and wall-eyed. He doesn't like Sabu, and Sabu is afraid of him.[1] Hard luck, isn't it!

Melkote.
October 5th.

Dear . . .

We are camped on the tip of a thousand-foot hill, overlooking an immense disc of plain to purple horizons that remind me of the Arizona desert.

---

[1] Not many months later, Lakshmi Prassad, going 'musth', killed a mahout who was walking in front of him.

Except for the new cloths of the famous weavers of *Melkote* Melkote, there seems to be nothing in all the village of sacred temples and sacred tanks that is less than five centuries old. When we came with our long train of elephants they told us that Tipu Sultan, a hundred and fifty years ago, had promised them that no elephant *We break a* should ever again come to Melkote. Now we had *Promise* broken that promise. So we paid the temple priest ten rupees (fifteen shillings). Also the people thought we were going to sacrifice a man to an elephant. But they are sweet people and have given us a romantic bathing place, one of their own sacred tanks, to bathe in.

But we were no sooner settled in Melkote than the *Little* rain came down; this time the little monsoon—a sort *Monsoon* of afterthought! We amused ourselves through the drizzling days riding on our elephants through the scrub bush high on the hills, looking for pig and panther.

The rain curtains over the plains were lovely. Sudden shafts of sunlight would shoot down through the rolling black clouds and spotlight patches of shining green plain. Down on that rolling plain beneath us was another sport—black buck. We might not shoot them for they were protected. But I longed to go out and see them. And one morning we did.

Darlings,

. . . It was almost too fairy-like for me to describe. We left camp by starlight. By dawn and the light of the morning star we were rolling over the plains, and somehow the great thundering dawn above us and the great stretching plain before us and, dwarfed to the finest dry-point etching between them, ourselves on our fantastic beasts, and the delicate leaping buck, were like nothing but a Persian miniature painting out of a fairy story.

Black Buck   The buck didn't know whether to be frightened. They sprayed from the hollow and capped the rise, every delicate line from hoof to head and horn flung up sharp and clear. And we rolled on after them for the sheer joy of seeing them leap again, up, up into the sky—beautiful curves shivering like glass the first rays of the sun. The lovely creatures didn't know what to think. They had never seen elephants before!

Irawatha, our Kala Nag, was very ill. He stood doubly chained by his forefeet and hind feet in a place by himself, and no one was allowed to come near him. He looked terrible and his eyes were wild with pain. He could not keep still. His head was never still but nodding and nodding and swaying and swaying, up and down and from side to side, and every once in

80

[*facing* IRAWATHA 'MUSTH']

a while he would lift his trunk up, up and let out a *Poor*
heart-rending cry. *Irawatha!*

Bob got out the cameras and filmed him. He had
the mahout throw him a bunch of leaves as though
urging him to eat, and Kala Nag, his head still swaying, swished it up in his trunk and swished it around
and finally threw it in a completely mad gesture over
his head, where it hung awry, like Ophelia's wreath.
This sounds funny, but actually in the film when we
ran it, it was quite as affecting as it was to see. The
poor elephant was most evidently in the depths of an
agony that made you feel very sorry for him.

Mysore. Nov....

Bob always has the luck. I told you, didn't I, that
our elephant, Irawatha, went ' Musth', and we could-
n't use him all the time we were in Melkote. It was an
ill wind that blew us plenty of good, for we took pictures of the poor creature in his painful, uneasy state,
and it made him look just as we want him to look in
the story when he is 'grieving for his master'!...

The film begins to look like something. The casting
is over and the first third of the picture, all the opening scenes, are shot. And now for our big dramatic
scenes in the jungles we are taking a fresh leap into
the unknown and incalculable.

PART II
NOVEMBER TO MAY
THE JUNGLE

Now we came to that part of our Indian experience *Jungle Camp* we had been waiting for, dreaming of since we dreamed of India at all, as all people do—of that strange, exotic, perhaps terrible, always exciting place they think of as the Indian jungle. All the rest of our film was to be shot in the jungle.

We had fixed upon our jungle location. It was Karapur. And thanks to the kind and generous Maharajah, we were to live at Karapur Camp in that same very comfortable guest bungalow that we had enjoyed before.

Our camp spread out from the lodge in rows of white tents. Everything was brought from Elephant House—bearers, cooks, cars, trucks—a bare skeleton was left behind—and we settled down in Karapur.

[*facing* IRAWATHA IS WELL AGAIN

Dearest . . . ,

The River   Oh, how I wish I could have you here in this
heavenly spot! The jungle all around us, the river below us, a blue sky above and everything bathed in
delicious sunlight, a cool breeze blowing and cold
nights. A fascinating film to do, a beautiful boy, and
an elephant to match, and so much besides that I am
distracted. One wants to sit by the river side all day
long and watch the river village people come and go;
a strip of shining beach, bamboo behind, river before
and these beautiful people out of a fable with their
slender, fine cattle, shining pots, flowing saris and
inimitable grace and graciousness. They are just getting water and washing themselves. But what a thing
to see!

This morning Captain Fremlin took me out in his
little boat. A couple of miles down the river and half a
mile up is our range, between swift waters and too
many rocks. It was lots of fun. We paddled down,
close to the shore, under the willows and bamboo.
Under the willows the carp, little and big, little
splashes and big splashes, were jumping for the fluffy
white seed-pods that drift down from them to rest
lightly on the water.

Captain Fremlin knows the river stretch well
enough now to know just what is there and where to
look for it. We saw a bronze fly-catcher and then a

wagtail. There was a wagtail, he said, that sat on a *The River* tiny knob of rock in midstream and poured its heart out in song. We came to the rock and there was the wagtail! and never have I heard a more thrilling song, not even a canary's. Another little wagtail stood quietly on the bank and never stirred as we came along, head cocked, entranced, listening. Kingfishers (so bright they made you gasp), plovers, doves, flights of them in the trees, all went about their business, and green flycatchers, paddy birds and 'Dill the Kite'.

A little farther down in a windfall of dead bamboo *Monkey Nursery* was what I am sure was a monkey nursery. I saw the tiniest baby monkeys I have ever seen, as though just born. It was an ideal retreat. And the whole tribe was in attendance.

I thought if I had young children again I should bring them up on this river and they would see the fabled kingfisher and the carp who swallowed the Princess's ring, and the story-book kite, and how much more fascinating the fables and the story books would be.

Farther down was another sight to see, a ferry; not *Elephant Ferry* the ordinary kind. The ferrying was done by two elephants. They hauled the bullock carts across, while the bullocks swam and the drivers rafted themselves on a bamboo raft. Cart after cart came down and the elephants plodded back and forth and back and forth; an old tusker and a little cow.

Mugger   A native boy hailed us from the bank, pointing down stream.

'Mugger!' exclaimed Captain Fremlin, 'and I didn't bring my gun.'

The mugger (crocodile) was sunning himself on a rock not much bigger than himself, for he was a big one. He slid into the water as we came along. We saw his snout for a moment at the surface and then he dived under. In this stretch of river the crocodiles are not man-eating. Fourteen miles farther down, they are; hereditary taste, they say.

Darling Mon,

Lone Wild   Great excitement in camp! A wild tusker is
Tusker! visiting our cows where they are tethered out at night. He is a fine specimen, half grown and extraordinarily bold. He came to the roadside the other morning and took a look at us. When Bob and Co. on a cow went up, most injudiciously, to take a nearer look, he stood his ground ready to charge. Muthanna[1] says that he is an outcast from the herd. A herd has one leading old tusker and a number of young ones. If a young one becomes insubordinate he is kicked out. To join the herd again he has to fight

---

[1]Muthanna was an officer of the Forest Service detailed to us by H.H. to look after us, keep us out of trouble—see that in our ignorance plus enthusiasm plus desperation-to-get-the-picture we did nothing rash.

88

[*facing* THE JEMADAR AND GOOD IRAWATHA WHOM HE CAPTURED WANDERING ALONE AND 'MUSTH' IN THE MYSORE JUNGLE

and overcome the leader. One night we thought our tusker had rejoined the herd, for he disappeared. But the following night he came back, so he probably had no luck. It is these outlaws, Muthanna says, whose tempers get sourer and sourer until they become the dreaded rogues.

The Jemadar has all his mahouts working preparing strands of hempen rope, twisting them together to the thickness of ships' cables. He wants to go out with his cows and rope that tusker.

Going up to a wild tusker in the jungle and putting a rope around his leg was a way of catching a creature, reputed to be the most dangerous of jungle animals, that I had never imagined. Was this some speciality of the Jemadar's? The impression was that since it *was* the Jemadar, it could be done. He had done it before. As a matter of fact it was in this way in these very jungles nine years before that he had caught Irawatha. Irawatha, the biggest tusker in Southern India, was his own single-handed catch. Now it was the rounded perfection of strength and audacity in this half-grown specimen of a potential 'rogue' that set all the Jemadar's elephant-catching nerves a-tingle.

The day appointed for the capture came. A special mahout had been sent for and had travelled all the way from up-country to be the Jemadar's right hand. The thick, heavy coils of rope were loaded on to five specially chosen cows. Five cows, laden with rope—nothing else—disappeared into the jungle.

We waited on the road. We were not to come in until after the Jemadar had the first rope around the tusker's leg and securely fastened to a tree. We waited, mounted on our elephants, ready to be called—15—20 minutes, a half hour—and then went in . . .

Never have I imagined such an animal scene. Aside from the struggles of the tusker uprooting bushes and knocking down a tree, and the clever way the mahouts tied him up, actually with one foot each on the tusker's back, it was the cow elephants that amazed me.

The root of the matter is elephant nature. A tusker will never attack a cow; it is the jungle law. And so the cows know that they can do with him what they will. And their law is to serve their master, the mahout. Leaning with all their weight one on either side of the tusker, they wedged him between them so that he couldn't move (of course he thought he was being made love to, anyway), they flapped their ears in his eyes, so that he wouldn't see the Jemadar crawling under his belly to get at his leg, and they jammed his legs so that he couldn't kick. The Jemadar was entirely at the mercy of his cows. Putting the first rope on the tusker's leg was considered so dangerous that, as I have said, we were not allowed to come into the jungle to see it.

The wild animal is so strong that it took five of these ships' cable ropes, from his hind legs, his fore- legs and neck, to hold him, and the ends of the ropes were wound round and round the middles of the five cows. The two cows attached to his hind legs faced backward so as to act as brakes. And so the poor gallant was led from his trysting place, a captive.

Now we had in our captured tusker, of course, an extraordinary film property. And we hastened to make the most of it, while the poor creature was still rebellious and fierce and before he should have become reconciled.

We had written into the story a scene for Kala Nag, very tentatively, for we didn't know how we were going to get it short of—well—very quick cutting of action staged with a tame elephant. As a matter of fact we had been experimenting with this scene, and, to use my husband's pet expression, been 'sweating blood'. Elephants are so incredibly slow and deliberate in their movements—so willing and intelligent, but so . . . deliberate. A tiger is a bundle of perfectly obvious ferocity—snarling lips and gleaming fangs and blazing eyes, lashing tail; he is the classic jungle villain. But what can you do with an elephant?—his little eyes, waving trunk, funny behind, silly tail, and a bulk that at any near distance appears on the screen simply as a blur of grey hide. For filming in action he

91

is the most peculiarly awkward material—were he
really on the go, one would hesitate to set up a
camera in his path.

This scene that we had written for Kala Nag was
an angry, tearing, raging mad one. The elephant loses
all self-control, breaks his picket, challenges the world
to come on and be smashed up, and then runs amok
and begins to smash everything in sight.

We had a long conference with Muthanna, and the
upshot was that there was great business for the
jungle men on a wooded hillside, building a camp,
the camp where Kala Nag is supposed to be tethered,
where he breaks away, and which he smashes up. To
this camp of bamboo huts the captured tusker was led
to play the part of the infuriated Kala Nag. Muthanna
promised us that he was in a furious mood.

It was exciting. He was tethered by ropes from
both hind legs to a tree and the ropes were about
sixty feet long so that he had a good range. The question, of course, was whether or not the ropes would
hold him and everything was arranged with a view to
a possible accident. The cameras were not in machans
where they would have been safe. The machans we
had had time to build were not steady enough. So
they were all fixed in a row on top of a high platform,
which would come down like so much matchwood if
the tusker ever got at it. Ladders were tied up to near-

[*facing* TAKING THE CAPTURED TUSKER TO WATER.
THE TWO KUMKIES IN THE FOREGROUND
ARE ACTING AS BRAKES TO KEEP THE TUSKER
FROM CHARGING THOSE IN FRONT

Photograph by Barbara Flaherty van Ingen

by trees for the camera crew to climb into in case of need, and Captain Fremlin, with his elephant gun, was stationed where he could cover their retreat.

Daddy was just prancing on his platform, cracking jokes about what might happen. There was a rope above the platform stretched across between two stout trees. This was Daddy's bright idea, so that if the cameras and all went down suddenly, the camera men could at least clutch on to the rope. Can you see Daddy dangling in mid air while an enraged tusker finishes up the cameras below?

Well, it didn't happen that way. The ropes held, and it was rather a pathetic scene. After plenty of smashing we called it off, for fear the poor tusker, straining and straining at his rope, would do himself in. He had taken one crashing fall.

Since then he has been cared for as tenderly as a precious creature could be. And every day we have a report as to how he is getting on. Yesterday he was not so well. To-day he is better. He is very wild, charging even the cows. He won't eat. He does eat. He can't sleep. He slept a little. They are doing their best to save him. But the truth is that very few tuskers survive capture for more than a short time. Of the eight our Jemadar has caught, our Irawatha is the only one now living.

There was one tusker bigger, more beautiful than Irawatha, with such a head as was never seen. For a

93

year and a half they nursed him and how well they nursed him you can imagine. Then one day someone took him out into his old jungle. It was too much for him. He came back to the stables and refused to eat, and died. It is a commonplace here that elephants die of a broken heart.

True Stories There are so many extraordinary elephant stories we hear at first hand. I was telling Mrs. Whitehead, wife of the Chief Conservator of Forests for Madras Presidency, how extraordinary I had found it to watch those cows at the capture of our tusker, as though, quite independent of the mahouts, they were doing the whole thing themselves. She said, yes, her husband had caught a mother and baby in a pit. The mother, after fighting frantically, just gave up and lay down a dead weight and they couldn't get her up. So they prodded the baby, which put her on her feet again raging, and they hauled her out. But she was in such a rage that the big tusker and two big cows, to which she was tied, couldn't hold her, and off she tore into the jungle, dragging them after her and spilling the mahouts.

Fortunately, as it happened, the leading rope caught in a tree and snapped with such suddenness that it threw the mother. So what did the tame tusker and cows do then, quite of their own accord, but turn and stand over the mother and not let her up, but held her there. And there they were when the mahouts

94

came up. And back they all came, the tusker in the *True Stories* lead as proud as punch.

Meanwhile the baby had been hauled out of the pit and tethered. It was bawling and bawling. They thought to hush it by letting it loose to go to the mother. But no, it just bawled and bawled. Whereupon the tusker, completely fed up, took the situation in hand, gave the baby one huge toss with his tusks and sent it hurtling through the air. The chastened baby picked itself up and rushed to mother.

She had another story, again about an elephant in a pit; this time another lonely, flirtatious tusker, like ours. Nightly he was allowed to visit his lady love over a well-worn path. Then a pit was dug under the path and guarding the pit at four corners were tethered four cows. The lady love was tethered at the far side.

Mr. Gallant came; saw one cow. No, she wasn't the one. Saw another. No, not she. Another and another . . . ah! There she was. And he made straight for his love and . . . into the pit. But it was night, and by night nothing could be done about roping him. And he began working with his tusks at the sides of the pit, crumbling the earth and stamping it under to build himself up and out of it. So Jubilee, a big tame tusker, was stationed at the pit edge to knock him back; which Jubilee did all night long. Jubilee's mahout had reason to thank Jubilee before the night was

Saved by out. He made a miss-step over the corner of the pit
Jubilee and was falling in when Jubilee's trunk shot out and
caught him back.

Some time before we moved to the jungle, David
had been sent to Assam to report on keddah operations and possible resources for our film over there.
Frances went with him. Her letter about the training
of the elephants after capture made me wish our
tusker might not have to go through such an ordeal
as she described.

Assam   Assam, on the banks of the Brahma Putra, they
found a dismal place, cold and wet and comfortless,
remote and wild.

First there was an incident at the stockade; where
they were watching the elephants being roped.

'David and I were perched on a narrow scaffolding
on top of the stockade with all the cameras and gear.
There was one full-grown tusker viciously using his
tusks, goring his neighbours. He would catch one of
them by the tail and bite it. At this the jungle men
raised a shout, for an elephant minus his handsome
tail fetches only half price. "Biddy, biddy," they cry.
"Don't, don't!" and brandish a torch or shoot off a gun.

'Well, as I say, we were there, busy with the cameras
taking snaps. Suddenly the stockade gave a lurch and
began to rock. I lost my balance and clutched at

96

[*facing* MOTHER ELEPHANT WITH BABY BORN
IN CAPTIVITY
Photograph by Barbara Flaherty van Ingen

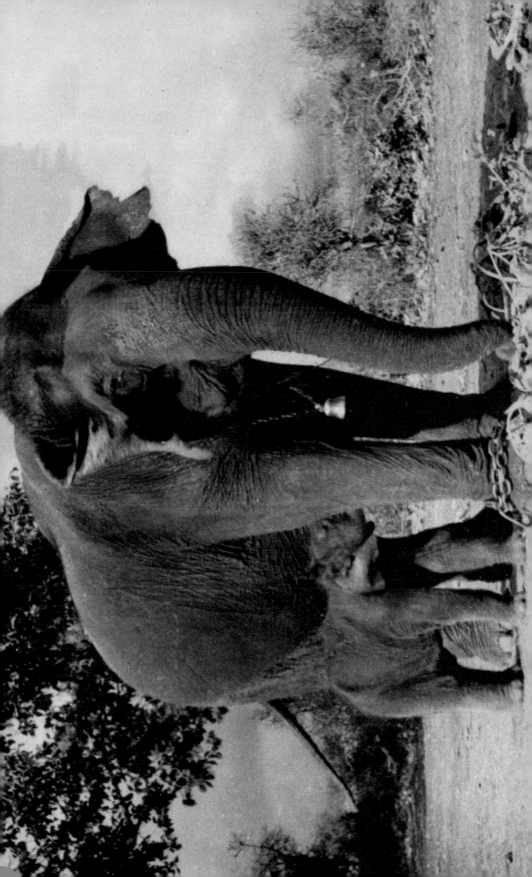

David just in time to save myself from falling over. *Assam*
The camera box did go over, down, crash! We
looked down. Directly beneath us the tusker, his
tusks wedged in the stockade posts, was shaking it
furiously to shake us off or shake the stockade down.
That was one nervous moment! Then someone flung
the stockade gates open wide, and off he went snort-
ing, tail in the air.'

Then the training—

'As we approached the depot at night for the first
time while still a mile off we could hear the trumpeting of the elephants, and, as we came nearer, the
chanting of the mahouts. It was an exciting sound.
We came into the depot, and it was lit like a vault
from underneath by a myriad of little fires which
were surrounded by squatting figures, behind which,
blending with the trunks of the trees, were the huge,
grey, shifting shapes of the elephants.

'We had come to watch the "night training" of a *Night*
twenty year old tusker caught that day and highly *Training*
bid for at the auction that afternoon. He was superb,
short but thick gleaming tusks, tremendously powerful shoulders and head, and his eyes—how can I ex-
plain it to you? . . . I had seen wild elephants at
every other stage of their capture and training, but
in this one I saw an elephant facing the fires, the
smell and the cunning of humans for the first
time.

G   97

'He was tied between two trees—stretched hind and
forefeet between them. Slowly a group of men approached with burning torches. The elephant recoiled,
because there is nothing that terrifies him more than
fire. He swung his head from side to side, his eyes
dilated and blood-shot, straining at the ropes; but the
men approached nearer until they were surrounding
him. Then they started chanting, and while one man
waved a torch up to his eyes, the others gently rubbed
his sides and legs with sticks. At first he was terrified,
then bewildered. The chanting, the continuous motion of the rubbing, and the fire swinging before his
eyes seemed to act like a drug. After half an hour or so
he began to sway drunkenly on his feet, righted himself, swayed again and tottered. As soon as he was
about to collapse the men stopped their chanting
abruptly, raised a shout and prodded him with their
long spears to startle him into a standing position
again, only to repeat the whole operation. It wore the
elephant out as nothing else could,—until after a few
hours they left him to rest.

'The training as it goes on by day is more kind. The
mahouts praise the sufferer. As he is marched up and
down and up and down between them they chant to
him; they praise his fine long tusks; they tell him of
the big jemadar who caught him, of the rich man who
will buy him, of the golden howdah he will wear one

98

day, and of the weddings and processions and fairs he will see—and fair women . . . '

There are elephants that are born and reared in cap- *Elephant* tivity, but these, I am told, never make the 'good' *and Man* elephants who work and obey and become the devoted life companions of their keepers that these wild ones do. For the essence of the relationship between the man and the animal is that the wild spirit has been broken—like a broken thing this strange, great heart in the queer great body clings for life to the only thing that is now left to it, its only security, this human who has taken it and made it his own.

Viceroy Lodge,
Karapur Camp.

Dearest Monnie,

I saw them building a shed to-day, down at the *Cowsheds are* bottom of the compound. What for? For our cows! *necessary* (We have about a dozen cows for our milk supply.) But why on earth, I wondered, should cows need a shed in a country like this? Don't tell me that all those hundreds of village cows that clutter up the road coming back at night from the jungle pastures to the villages are all put up in sheds? Why? Panther, of course; or tiger. A tiger took a cow just down the road from us only the other night. The tiger Bordie is baiting, to kill it, has taken twenty cows from one village alone in two months.

Cowsheds are
necessary   Sabu thinks he sees panther stealing in the compound and taking off pie dogs almost every night.
It's the way the Jemadar gets him to go to bed, and
keep well under the covers!

'Rogue'   It sometimes comes over me to marvel how casu-
Elephant   ally and matter-of-factly we live here and go about.
Never a time do we start out on a jungle adventure
that we are not regaled with the most awful tales of
the danger and ferocity of the elephant in its wild
state, particularly the *rogue* who actually lies in
wait for the unwary and tears him limb from limb,
and stamps him to pulp or tosses him into a tree—
oxen, carts, men.

One attacked a motor car a few days ago. Rounding
a turn, the occupants of the car saw the elephant
standing in the road some distance off. From the way
he cocked his ears they knew he meant business. The
elephant made for the car and the occupants abandoned it and got away. The elephant made a thoroughly good job of wrecking the car. In a few mo-
ments it was a heap of scrap. Unfortunately for the
elephant the radiator got jammed on his tusks and off
he went into the jungle wearing it!

Now came the question how were we to go about
getting at the herds of elephants in the forest to film
them. There were plenty of herds there—the jungle
men were on the lookout for them, reporting every

[*facing* THE JEMADAR. OUR MAHOUTS AND THEIR
ELEPHANTS LOVED, FEARED AND OBEYED
HIM

day what they had seen and where. They were watch- *Wild herd*
ing two herds. One of these they reported to be of *located*
extraordinary size with an extraordinary number of
young tuskers—tuskers about the size of our captured one—probably the herd from which he had
been ousted. A party was made up to go out and
see it.

Yesterday I had the very greatest thrill of my life,
probably because we are so filled up with wild elephant tales. We went out to see the wild herd; on
three cows, our cow leading, with Captain Fremlin
sitting in front with his gun; three trackers taking us *We visit it in*
to where they were, trotting along ahead. The Jema- *the Jungle*
dar on the last elephant had a whistle for signalling.
Through a tall, dark teak stand, the high grasses
trampled on every hand, we came into a feathery
forest of tender green bamboo and to a nullah with
pools of water still in it.

Young bamboo shoots and water spell elephants.
We were on them before we knew it. The Jemadar
whistled for us to look where we were going. We
had not seen him until he stood there, large enough
and near enough to be frightening, for he was
HUGE, and he had the longest, sharpest pointed
tusks I have ever seen. Still we went nearer, God
knows why, thought I. The creature turned and faced
us and his head framed in the green jungle growth

(black head and gleaming tusks) was the most massive thing I have ever seen.

What was he going to do now that he had seen us?
Why on earth didn't he turn away? Captain Fremlin
took his gun in hand and whispered to me, reassur-
ingly, that if he had to shoot him it would be a damn
difficult shot! We did turn, and I kept looking over
my shoulder. What was my horror to see that the
tusker was following us, coming exactly in our path
like a dog following its master, or a master of the
harem following his cows, *our* cows! Was it curiosity? Or had he taken it into his head to charge
us?

Then my attention was distracted by a beautiful
sight—in silhouette against the light green foliage—
three does with enormous ears, and the magnificent
head and neck of a stag. Sambhur!

And then all at once I began seeing them. One's
eye has to be accustomed for there wasn't a sound,
but goodness, there they were right under our noses,
hidden, half hidden in the grass and trees. On one side
of us there was an enormous cow. She paid no apparent attention to us. But on the other side was a bunch
of young tuskers. We saw six of them. They were
watching us. We stood stock still. They began
knocking each other about, running and squealing,
having a frolic or a scrap. They were six replicas of
our caught wild tusker. I am sure he was one of their

brothers. An angry trumpeting came from further ahead and on another side other great beast sounds. We had wandered squarely into the middle of the herd and were completely surrounded. Might they not close in on us? Muthanna said afterwards that they might have done. We turned back on our path, on the same path down which the tusker had been following us. Where was he by now? The big cow to the left of us still took no heed. (We heard afterwards that she was calving.) The three trackers were trotting ahead, when the Jemadar's low warning whistle sounded again. The trackers fell back and we all stopped while something crashed off into the bushes. He was standing behind a bush by the path, Muthanna said, when the Jemadar saw him. Muthanna said he was waiting there to waylay us.

How the Jemadar would like to catch that herd in a keddah. But he can't. No keddah could hold a herd like that with all those tuskers. Such a herd was never seen here before. But we can try to drive them through a clearing and take pictures from machans.

These forests had been the scene of many famous elephant drives or 'keddahs', superbly organized. All through the forest were forest huts and forest rangers experienced and seasoned to the work. Four miles from Karapur was Mastagudy, the elephant camp,

103

with twenty elephants. Four miles beyond that in the forest were the ditches, post holes and rotting timbers of the old keddahs still standing.

Just how we finally came to the decision, I don't know. It seemed to grow out of the circumstances. That magnificent wild herd such as had hardly been seen here before; the old keddah sites, so easy to reconstruct, all there; the forestry organization just ready to be set in motion; and, above all, the certainty of getting our pictures in this way as in no other—all these things conspired together. We decided to have a keddah, a real keddah in the traditional style; to call all the villagers from miles around to make a small army (1,100, actually) of beaters, to pair these with jungle men, and to call out the forest officers to captain this army: to build the stockade and runways—an engineering feat of timber (10,000 pieces) and rope (9 tons); of digging and chopping and hauling—with hundreds of carts and all the work-elephants engaged. It sounded like a tremendous undertaking for just a film. A keddah is staged in Mysore only after many months of preparation and only for one most important occasion—the visit to Mysore of a new viceroy or of royalty.

The habits and seasonal movements and runways of the elephants are well known, and the keddah operators take account of these. The river runs through the

[*facing* THE STOCKADE GATE, MADE TO SWING UP
LIKE A TRAP AND CRASH DOWN AT THE
CUTTING OF A ROPE

area and they know when the elephants may be expected to cross.

The area is about sixty miles square. In it there are ten forest lodges with rangers. And scattered through it by twos or tens are about eight hundred Kurubars or jungle men, who live in grass and bamboo shelters on wild honey and roots. They are used for the elephant drives only in company with villagers, because, left alone, they are afraid of elephants and at sight of a wild herd will scramble into trees—probably because the wild elephants trample and destroy their huts. Though they look like nothing but long, slender bones covered with black skin, they are very strong.

We are building our keddah on one of the two traditional keddah sites in a dense bamboo thicket between the road and the river. The line of the enclosures—an inner stockade seventy-five feet in diameter, and leading into it another about six hundred feet long—is being pricked out in enormous holes to receive the timbers which are being brought in by train after train of bullock carts. In about two weeks' time, Muthanna says, everything will be ready.

From this time on the plot thickened. It was only a few days to Christmas. As soon as the stockade was finished, the wild herd would be surrounded and held by the beaters until time for the drive. The area within which a herd is held is called a 'sur-

The beaters'
job round'; the beaters who hold it—stationed twenty to thirty feet apart all around it—are the 'lines'. It is the beaters' job to watch that there is no move on the part of the herd to break through; day and night they hold the lines with fire and bamboo clappers—pieces of bamboo split to clap together and make a sharp noise.

The 'Lines' It was Christmas Eve just at midnight that Frannie and I, coming from Mysore, had our first sight of the 'lines'—the beaters around their fires, with their bamboo clappers. As we came along they delightedly gave us a demonstration of the noise that they could make, clapping and yelling out to the elephant herd somewhere in the eerie black stillness of the jungle.

We had surrounded the big herd; the beaters were holding them there. On the banks of the river we had put up machans for our cameras. And the first thing we were going to do was to drive the herd past them into the river and across it. There we would again surround them and hold them until we were ready to drive them again, this time back across the river, into our stockade. The stockade was ready. It had been built of 10,000 logs and nine tons of rope. Beyond the runway wings extended along the river bank (see diagram, page 115). The two gates at the entrances of the stockade and runway were gigantic things, specially constructed to swing up like a trap, and crash down by cutting a rope.

The beaters drive on foot, of course, with no *The Drive* weapons—only the bamboo clappers to make a noise. They are supported by foresters with shot-guns, and by 'kumkies', tame elephants—about twenty of them —which come along behind them. I wished very much to be riding one of those elephants instead of being stuck up in a machan. But I had to stay with the cameras.

Early on the day of the first, the preliminary drive, we took our places. It was exciting even at the machans. Bob had to be moved from a very shaky, rotten tree to a safe one. The trees have to be strong enough to withstand an angry tusker's charge and the machans have to be high enough to be out of his reach.

Our machan was right over the runway; it wasn't big enough for all of us, so I hoisted myself into a crotch of the tree. Finally we were all settled high and safe, and Muthanna went off to call the drive. We were all prisoners in our trees, of course, until he came back again to let us down, or, as we expected, until the elephants had passed. We were cautioned that from the time we heard the bugle announcing the coming of the herd, we must be absolutely still. I was glad there was a bugle. I love the sound of a bugle; it is peculiarly exciting.

Whatever was going to happen would be beyond *First Day of* our ken in the jungle behind us. Captain Fremlin and *Preliminary Drive*

Sabu were back there on an elephant following the
beaters. The Captain carries the only heavy gun, the
special elephant gun. We could only guess of what
was going on by the sounds that came, nearer or
farther, of yelling, clapping, occasional shots and the
bugle call.

Nothing happened. At five o'clock Muthanna
came to relieve us. Captain and Sabu had had a
grand time inside the lines. Besides the elephant herd
they had scared up sambhur, cheetah, bison, pig, a
mouse-deer, and plenty of langoors. Chasing around
inside the lines with the Jemadar, six kumkies and
twenty beaters, they had had a lovely time, but there
had been no organized drive. Muthanna was very
angry with the Jemadar.

Three days . . . no luck. Three days of just sitting in
a machan all day—and just wait until you try that for
fun. Nibbling biscuits and sandwiches; watching the
birds coming to the river to drink and teetering on
their little tails; going to sleep, reading, writing,
drowsing.

Suddenly something like an electric shock went
through us, running from one to the other; we
straightened up, breath caught in the middle, strained
our eyes over the placid river, along the empty shores,
into the shadowy forest-fringe, trying to see. There he
was! But on the wrong side of the river, coming
from the opposite shore! An enormous tusker just

108

[*facing* LAKSHMI, PRIZE WORK ELEPHANT OF THE
KAKANKOTE CAMP, PUTTING UP THE GATE
POST FOR OUR STOCKADE

coming out into the open, alone. Almost trembling we watched him come down the bank, and step into the river. He was crossing it!

Quickly cameras clicked and whirred, but only for a moment. Then tall rushes and low willows hid him. Making for the forest behind us, he disappeared. Then just birds again, and no sound from behind where the drive was supposed to be going on. Once we heard the bugle and shots and yelling, but then all faded away again. So we knew something was going wrong. Apparently everything had been going beautifully—all the wild herd rushing for the run, the Jemadar driving on one wing, Muthanna on the other, Captain Fremlin in the centre—when suddenly everything happened at once. Two big cows with calves turned and broke through the beaters who tumbled every which way. And out of the bushes, a monstrous tusker came charging straight at Fremlin. He gave him a shot, and saw the elephant lurch drunkenly from the shock.

The tusker was charging not Fremlin's cow but the tame tusker behind him. But for Fremlin's lucky shot, the wild tusker would have killed the tame one and his mahout, and then turned on the beaters. Muthanna says the beaters are all heroes. The forest officers with them have shot-guns. As the beaters drive, the foresters keep their eyes on the wild tuskers. If one shows signs of slackening, they give him a volley of shot before he has a chance to turn and make trouble. Once he turns, it is time to shoot to kill. As I have said before there is only one vital place to kill an elephant, a spot four inches square just between the eyes. Fremlin's shot went high, into the spongy bone above. It was the power of the gun, the force of the shot, that stopped the charge. There is little doubt that this tusker was the one we saw crossing the river!

Between the river where our machans were and the forest behind us where the elephants were and from which we were trying to dislodge them, ran a road—the highway. We now came to the conclusion that it was this road that was making the difficulty, that the herd was refusing to cross this road—and could not, probably, be driven across it in the daytime.

So we hatched another scheme. Instead of driving them across the river and filming them there, we would drive them across an open glade in the jungle and film them there.

For this we had to put up machans again, this time inside the lines. Bob and the carpenters went out early in the morning. I had orders to follow at noon. Then it was reported that lunch would be served in the jungle and if we wanted it we were to get it there. So out we went, plus two guests.

We came to two korumba guides waiting for us by

the roadside. We struck into the jungle behind them. As we jogged along, every once in a while my guide would let out a volley of talk as though to himself, until I discovered that every few feet there was a korumba lodged in a tree. The talk between them sounded very business-like. We crossed a marshy place where the black mud was an immense honeycomb of fresh elephant tracks. I was relieved when at last we came to Bob and the others.

Our reception wasn't cordial. We weren't expected, nor was the elaborate lunch of hors d'oeuvres, hot curry and what not, being served out of an enormous box by all our bearers. However, there we were, right in with the wild elephants. Captain Fremlin ate his lunch with his gun ready loaded at hand. The three kumkies were stationed around us facing out into the jungle, in three directions, to give the alarm should any of the wild herd appear. While we sat and ate I saw my jungle guide regarding us fools of white men sitting there eating with an expression of the most supreme contempt. Quaint luncheon party!

Finally everyone cleared away and we were in our machans. Ours was directly in the sun and was it hot? Again the drive would seem to be coming and then fall away again, and again nothing happened. At four o'clock Muthanna came rushing up to transfer us to our old machans by the river. The herd was going to cross. Quick! quick! Before it would be too late to get a picture!

So pretty soon we were up in our old stand looking out across the river. And *again* it was from the *other* side of the river that the first alarm came; this time a big cow with a toddling baby behind her, and her three-year-old son, his little tusks just sprouting, behind the baby. She was a grand sight. Then the light failed. Dusk. No more chance for pictures. Still we had to sit there. We thought we heard crashing in the bushes behind us. We did. But again the alarm came from the other side; a tusker this time come down to drink. He stood there by the river edge until it grew so dark that we could no longer distinguish him.

It was quite dark when we heard something big in the river exactly in front of us, and gradually splash, splash, nearer and nearer. A huge form with sudden gleams of white tusks came straight toward us, looming larger and larger. Then from both our machans we broke out clapping, yelling, turning the old fellow back and splash, splash, now louder and faster, back he went on his tracks.

At eight o'clock came the relief. What had happened to the drive? Again the herd had balked at the road. A few had ventured to cross; that is what we had heard in the bushes. But again two cows had broken back, charging the kumkies. The Captain's elephant had bolted, but fortunately in open jungle.

112

[*facing* THE JUNGLE RIVER—VILLAGERS COME FOR
WATER AND TO BATHE

But now the herd was so closely surrounded that to *End of Preliminary Drive* get water they would have to make a break somehow. They would not be allowed to break back through the jungle so they would probably break towards the river and cross it during the night, and that is exactly what they did.

All that trouble and no pictures. Still our objective was achieved. The elephants were now across the river on the side where we wanted them.

There are still half a dozen elephants left wandering on this side. They were found when the country was scoured after the big herd had crossed in the night. But it was thought wiser to leave them alone. They were the trouble-makers in the drive; two big cows with two young, and a big tusker.

But we are not allowed to forget them. Last night, *Stray* Muthanna, with Cape and Bland,[1] found themselves *Elephants at* inside the stockade with the tusker just outside. And *the Stockade* evidently he was watching them. For when they moved he was still. When they were still he moved. The beaters with their fires were along the river bank. A bit of shouting brought them to the rescue. The tusker evidently wanted to cross the river to join the herd. He is conversant now with the stockade. My question is, if he did get across now would he spread the alarm and spoil the drive? Muthanna says if he is the *leader* of the herd he undoubtedly would.

[1]Our two sound engineers.

H   113

But no wild elephant has been known to face fire, hence the fire lines. The only animal, Bob says, that isn't afraid of fire is the bull moose. He will charge it, even charge the headlights of a locomotive.

The Stockade made stronger Our keddah has grown from a 'chance' keddah on a small scale to the traditional large-scale organized 'drive'; all on account of these big tuskers in the herd, and so many of them. It is evidently a very rare thing to have so many tuskers. In one keddah of eighty elephants caught only one was a tusker and he not so very big. Hence the renewed hammering and business at the stockade.

They are busy reinforcing it, driving a second row of uprights and buttressing them all around. Also they are hollowing out enormous logs of a wood that is water tight for drinking troughs to water the elephants in the stockade. The stockade is on one of the paths by which the elephants cross the river. All the other paths or runways for a mile on either side have been barricaded, as also any place in the bank not steep enough to form a natural barricade. The lay of the land is really ideal. It is ideal for us that this is all traditional work, too.

Origin of Mysore Keddah The origin of these keddahs was with Sanderson, sixty odd years ago, when he was Forest Officer for Mysore. He introduced keddah catching, which he learned in Assam. His book is the classic on the subject. But it was Muthanna's father some time in the

114

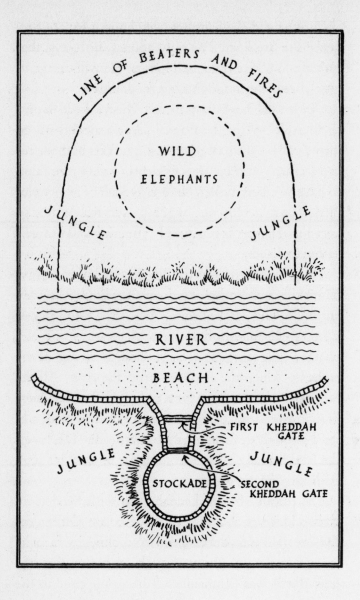

'90's who established the keddahs for what they are
and have been ever since—a spectacle organized to
the day and hour, such as can be seen nowhere else in
the world. And these keddahs were held for each new
viceroy—Mysore's unique way of showing honour
to a vice-regal guest. That is why this lodge we are
living in is called Viceroy Lodge. The Maharajah's
own bungalow, just next door, isn't half so imposing.

The last keddah was held in 1929 for Lord Irwin.
There were two thousand guests. The Viceroy's suite
alone numbered five hundred. The road from Mysore
was specially paved for the occasion and all traffic was
held up during operations. Unfortunately, the guests
made too much noise. Half way across the river the
elephants turned, frightened, upset the beaters and the
driving elephants and broke back into the jungle. It
was ten days before they were rounded up and driven
again.

The old days before motor cars were very picturesque. Everyone came in carts drawn by bullocks,
'trotting bulls', a special and famous Mysore breed.
The Maharajah still keeps a few of them. With these
bullocks the native troops could move faster than
the English with their horses. Captain Wellesley, the
future Duke of Wellington, was the first of the English to use bullock transport. The bullocks 'trotted'
at eight miles per hour. Every ten miles along the way
was a fresh relay. Quaint!

[*facing* ONE, TWO! LEFT, RIGHT!

Prince Jaya has sent a portable wireless truck down, *Prince Jaya's*
so that he can have daily reports of our opera- *Wireless*
tions and rush down in time to see the elephants
come in.

This morning we went up to Sanderson's Hill along *Preparations*
the lines. The line is seven miles around, the area a *for the*
rough triangle. The fires, which almost touch each *Big Drive*
other, are kept smoking. The beaters have built lean-
to's for themselves. The forest officers have little shelters, bamboo beds, tables, looking very inviting. How
beautiful the jungle was in the fresh morning, the
white, silvery mist still caught in the cobwebs. We
passed along the river behind enormous boles of trees.
The height of the jungle is impressive, particularly the
great height of the bamboos, when you think that
they are really only enormous grasses. They are as
weird as the elephants. The light in the jungle is never
too glaring, the sun never too hot; no flies, no mos-
quitoes, no noxious insects; a paradise compared to
camping country anywhere else in the world.

The Jemadar has set Saturday for the day of the
drive. There is no auspicious day before then. Friday
is the Mohammedan Sunday, holy day. He will offer
up prayers on Friday. For these people everything
must be 'auspicious'. And one can never tell when or
where auspiciousness is going to crop up. Muthanna
couldn't get a group of seven beaters from a certain

117

village to stay in a certain place. It was not auspicious for them.

Preparations for the Big Drive A heap of stones along the lines to-day marked the place of a god. Bob is giving money for a 'puja' there, and it makes them very happy. They all looked contented and happy cutting fire-wood, nursing their fires, cooking their rations. They get a ration of ragi a day—four to five annas worth—and their wage is six to eight annas (ninepence) for a twenty-four hour day. The doctor was going his round as we came down. Many of them were stretched out for their noon-day sleep. We are having a medal struck off to give them. It is a tradition; every keddah has had a medal. Ours will have on one side Sabu on Irawatha's head, on the other a camera and tripod.

Captain Fremlin says the organization is excellent.

So now our surround was on the side of the river were we wanted it. It was seven miles around. Inside it there was no water for the elephants—they would have to come to the river to drink. Opposite two places where they were most likely to come we set up the cameras. It was impossible to tell when they might come; we must just be ready—man the cameras from daylight to dusk. It was rather lovely spending the days camping on that wonderful river shore, waiting for our game.

Wild elephants playing in the water like children, right in front of our noses, at intervals to-day, an hour at a time, and we have missed it all, practically, simply by not being there. Cooper and Schmidt were there. But neither of them know enough about the cameras to make the most of an opportunity like that. Schmidt saw a daddy tusker push a baby into the water. What a shot!

To-day, all day long, we have not left the cameras —hoping for the herd to come to the river to drink and bathe and play, as they did yesterday. Our cameras are mounted on platforms, camouflaged, on the foreshore of the river. Lined along the high bank behind us were the beaters beside their fires, to keep the herd from crossing. Should they start to cross we were to film as long as possible and then run as fast as possible for the bank and up it until out of reach. It was too steep for the elephants to climb. It looked too steep for *anyone* to climb. I picked out a spot with plenty of tree roots sticking out for a hand hold.

Probably we hardly realize what a sight it is to see those elephants. Muthanna realized it. There are forest rangers who live their lives in the forest, he says, and are lucky ever to see an elephant at all. No one here ever saw such a sight before. The herd come to the river because there is no water in the surround. If there were only full grown elephants they would come at night. But there are a lot of babies and it is better for them to bathe while the sun is still up.

Jan. 1st.

Sid has just come in from the location. The elephants have already been bathing this morning (10.30). The big tusker came down first. Slowly, majestically, deliberately, he came down lifting his trunk, testing the air in every direction. All clear. So back up the bank he went and signalled. And then down through the screen of bamboo jungle they drifted, the big cows and the babies, the tusker standing to let them pass and then coming on behind. A baby got too far into the water. Out came daddy's trunk and pulled him on to the bank and laid him flat. If we could only get little things like that into the picture!

Yesterday we waited for them until we were ready to give up. Six o'clock. The sun was almost setting. Sh . . . Muthanna, with his fingers to his lips. After our whole day of waiting here they were coming at last. First the big tusker, as usual.

I opened my big lens out to the last stop (2.3). He stood on the bank half hidden by the bushes and all we could see was his trunk raised above them, this way and that, feeling the air. I was sure he would get our scent. The wind had died down. It had been favour-

120

able to us all day. Now there were currents going every which way. Yes, he had turned up the bank. The game was up. He had smelled us.

But no. Half way up the bank he paused and then. . . . The jungle screen along the river became alive, and drifting out of it and down the bank came the herd, more and more, until we counted more than fifty.

I was glad my lens was so fast. Still the light was terribly flat. The young elephants and babies sported in the water, their black heads bobbed up and down on the surface. The bank was steep and they climbed up on their knees and slid down on their haunches (by this time it was too dark to shoot any more so I just watched them), while three enormous cows stood guard on the bank, watching the children and throwing dust over themselves.

The big tusker came wading along up river and told them it was time to get back. A younger tusker remained behind, long after the herd had disappeared —though his little sweetheart waited for him just at the jungle edge—and though we dismounted our camera and packed up and made no bones about noise, he was still there, keeping watch, when we left.

But I forgot the bison—a magnificent bull, bold in the protection of the elephants—drinking his fill from the river, while his mate waited in the long grass where we could just see her horns. He drank and

Bison! drank without raising his head—it must have been ten minutes.

January 3rd. The Day Before the Big Drive.
10 a.m.

The Night before the Big Drive All set up by the riverside, opposite the place where the wild herd come to drink and bathe. Yesterday at this time Bob got 1,200 feet of them. Crazy to get some more. Priceless stuff. Waited all yesterday afternoon. But they came half a mile up river across from the stockade, where we had laid sugar cane. Laid sugar cane there, because we want them to come there for the drive.

But they were wary of the bait, and by the time we could move the cameras up they were gone, all except one tusker munching away. We watched him until he, too, turned up the bank. Still we waited and watched, aware by the agitation of the bamboo tops and occasional crashing that the herd was still there. Also, by sudden alarms from up river, clapping and yelling and flaring of fires, that they were pressing on that wing.

'They'll have a devil of a time on that line to-night,' one of the foresters opined.

Visit Lines by Night So when, about 10 p.m., we were ready to set out with Muthanna on his nightly round of the lines (this was the last night), I thought we were in for some fun. It *was* fun, if only for the sight of ourselves on

122

three enormous, moving, black shadows, silhouetted in the light of a hundred glimmering fires as we stepped over them, threading the 'line'.

Clapping and yelling behind us announced our coming to those before, so that those ahead should not be caught napping. But how soundly they slept! Twice we stepped over a sleeping form, lying across the path, wrapped head and all in the single cloth they wear.

'Lazy one, that can only eat and sleep, why don't you attend to your fire?' our mahout called down from his high seat, and as Rajpeary's huge pads so gently and carefully stepped over them, they might be glad it wasn't a ruder awakening. They have been watching now, night and day, for eight days.

And how hard to believe that there was anything in that soft, sweet jungle beyond, sweet with the smoke of sandalwood. For there is nothing sinister about the jungle, not so much so as in those dark, witch-like forests of Germany. It is all sweet and kind. Among the trees, so tremendously tall, stretching upward, we might have been in a cathedral. I cannot understand these fierce hunters with their tales of ferocious experience. As Bob said, he felt like a murderer watching that charming domestic scene of the wild families at the river side, thinking what a bad time we are going to give them, when all they ask is to be let alone in their paradise. The elephant has no living thing to fear but man. Probably that is why so often one comes upon other game near an elephant herd—bison and sambhur. They are there for protection.

As we came back to cross the river, a thin, milky mist was over it, making it look ghostly in the moonlight. The half moon mirrored in black pools between the rushes, and picked out in shining circles the slow swirl of sluggish currents. Like watchful, crouching eyes, the red gold fires along the bank were doubled in the water. A salvo of clapping came from them as our big beasts stepped out into view.

And the next day was the Day of the Big Drive. Operations started at 6 a.m. The actual 'rush' was not due to start—at a given signal—until 3 p.m.—3 *sharp*. Bordie had to be safe-conducted to his place in a machan inside the lines. Fremlin with his elephant gun was the safe escort. For when putting up the machan the big tusker had appeared. There was a distinctly nervous moment. The mahouts called to Fremlin to shoot. They clapped and yelled and the tusker turned away.

As we came down the road, two hours later, the morning mist was still in the air like fine rain. From Mastigudy, the elephant camp, the seven cows picked for the drive were just starting off to cross the river, where the beaters were waiting their coming to begin the day's manoeuvres. First the eastern wing was to be

[*facing* '. . . THE BOY WE IMAGINED']

moved up over half the area, the beaters carrying fire-
wood with them to establish a new line. This done,
the shikari elephants would move up to the apex of
the two lines, and the final drive, straight through to
the river, would begin.

From 2 p.m. our orders were to be in our machans,
absolute silence, no smoking. Over-night, our
machans and the stockade had been camouflaged;
elephants had been tethered all about to destroy the
scent of man. Elephants neither see well nor hear
well. (How much more careful we had to be with
crocodiles. You just knew that across the whole
width of the river they could see and were watching
every move.) The elephant depends on his trunk,
scenting the air.

Our machan was crawling with red ants, stinging
beasts, almost as bad as bees, and was exposed to the
sun without shade of branch or twig. Impossible! We
stayed out of it to the last minute. At one o'clock
Bordie abandoned his post inside the lines, without a
shot, alas, and came over with the news that the herd,
numbering eighty, was at the foot of Sanderson's
Hill, way up from the river. But by three o'clock we
could hear them coming . . . shouting, clapping,
shots . . . volleys of shots and the clear, high, exciting
'wind' of the bugle . . . staccato explosions of shots. It
sounded like a battle. It came directly at us with a rush.

Our big lenses were pointed, like machine guns, at

the shore, raking it up and down, not to miss the
first rush breaking cover. Then bang, bang! There
they came. But only for a moment, half a moment.
They turned down stream *out of sight, out of sight* they
crossed the river below us, and before we could even
change our lenses, before we could think, there they
came pounding along directly under our machan, a
bellowing, lurching sea of rushing backs, pouring into
the stockade. A complete rout, alas, for our cameras.
Behind them came the yelling beaters, brandishing
their torches.

Saturday, January 4th.

The drive is over and eighty elephants, as near as
we can count, are in the stockade. And two enormous
tuskers. The most spectacular herd ever driven, and
driven exactly to schedule, a triumph for Muthanna.
But what a pitiful sight to see them, their panic just like
the panic of a crowd of people, all regardless of each
other in their one idea of safety for themselves at the
centre of the milling circle, butting, pushing, jabbing
each other, and making terrible noises, groaning and
sobbing like the tortures of hell. Many of them show
buckshot wounds. The big tusker has a raw hole behind his eye; a big cow's eye is blind with blood.
There are several babies, one tiny one; probably the
baby to whose birth we were almost witness when
we visited the herd where they stayed in cover so

126

long. For it is the same herd we saw. The big tusker is the one that gave me such a thrill. Another tusker, almost as big, they say, is one that has been caught before; there are old rope marks on his legs. He is a 'bad one', therefore. But the tusker Fremlin had to shoot evidently did not belong to the herd.

They are putting on a wretched show now. Every once in a while a maddened mother, with a high, piercing trumpet, will charge the stockade. But not the tuskers; they are not at all brave and use all their tusks and weight to hold the centre place and jab the lesser ones away. I am so afraid the babies will get crushed. They are sweet little fellows. I heard Captain Fremlin say: 'Shall I shoot the poor creature?' A half-grown tusker was down in the mud on his side. By this time the whole stockade was a slimy, slippery mass of black mud like a stye, and smelling to heaven just like a stye.

Sunday Morning.

A baby goes down in the slippery mud of the stockade, under those huge milling bodies. It will be trampled. The Jemadar won't allow it; goes into the stockade, ropes the baby and pulls it to the barrier and they get it through. The little fellow isn't hurt, full of beans, and oh, how thirsty. It can't drink with its trunk, too young, but there's water on the ground and water in a shallow dish, and its silly little trunk

We Retrieve wobbles and splashes and tries to find its mouth. 'Oh,
the Baby how I'd like a good drink!'

We catch its trunk up and open its mouth and nearly choke the little creature pouring water down its
throat. But still with its funny little trunk pressed
down in wrinkles into the mud, it tries to get the rim
of the bowl in its mouth. It is too funny. The brown
faces watching are a study. They do love the little
thing. They start leading him, protesting, to the river.
At the river brink: 'No, I won't go in. I won't go in
without mother. Mother said not to go in without
her.' But once in, oh boy, what a long, happy drink.
'Now I've had enough. Let's go back to mother.' The
poor mother, as it passed the stockade, had followed
it around.

Tuesday, January 7th.

End of It is all over. The elephants are gone back to their
Keddah lovely jungle, the beloved beasts.

The I hated to come down to the stockade to face hear-
Elephants ing again their unceasing moaning and groaning from
are set free the depths of their agony and torture. It seemed to me
the sounds were worse, more despairing. The sudden
screams seemed like the last extreme of endurance.
They were human cries. They were like the boar
whose dying agony has rung in my ears all these
years. It was unbearable. We all broke down. Three
o'clock was set for the opening of the gates to let

128

[*facing* . . . AN AVALANCHE OF BODIES IN A
ROLLING CLOUD OF DUST . . .'

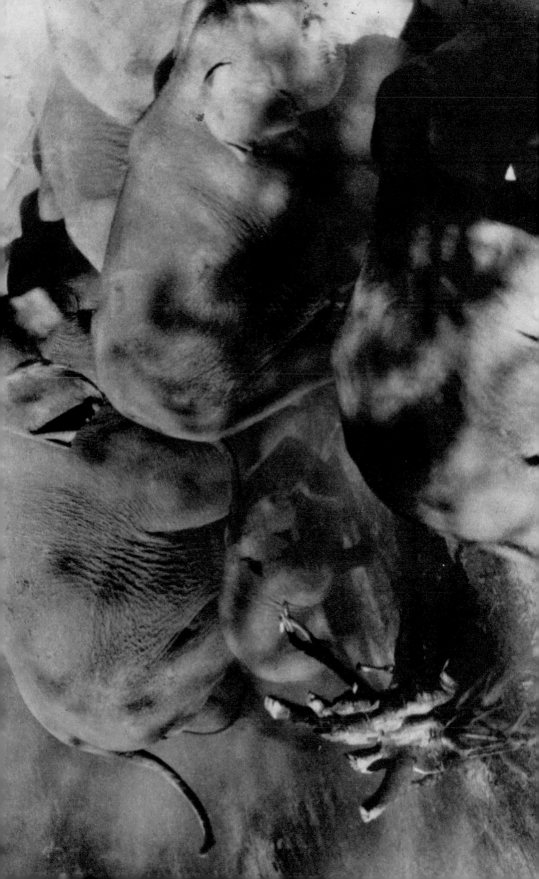

them go, set them free. Such a relief; I had to turn away into the bushes to hide that I was crying.

The baby is O.K. At first I thought he was dead, stretched out on his side, asleep But it was just as sweet and peppy as ever, the centre of an admiring, loving crowd, bringing it milk and water. But what to do with it? The herd, even the mother, now that it smelled of humans, would not take it back, would probably kill it. It might be raised by hand, it might be fostered by our tame mother cow elephant, sent up to her to the palace stables. A woman came and poured water over it from her shining brass pot. The baby wallowed delightedly in a puddle of water and mud.

Throwing bundles of straw and rice into the stockade and watching eager trunks reach out was some consolation. They crowded to the barriers to pick them up, even the big tusker became a hungry baby.

Everyone was having a guess as to what the elephants would do, once the gate was open—whether they would come in a rush or come slowly, whether they would stop at the water and drink, whether they would take the deep water crossing straight ahead or shepherd the babies to the shallows at one side.

And there was our baby, being brought down and let loose right under our machan. Perhaps, we thought, the herd in its excitement would take it along, perhaps the mother would find it. The little

thing instinctively wandered up into the enclosure
and along to the stockade to find mother where he
could hear her voice, I suppose, among the others. If
it stands there by the stockade gate, I thought, it's the
end. He'll surely be crushed in the first out-rush.

The tension during the final clearance of the runway under our machans I can hardly describe. A fifteen minute call before the gate was opened. Are you
ready? Yes. Frannie and I were on a low machan. I
was warned to draw my dangling feet up for fear the
big cow might spot me and try to mount our tree.
She had tried to climb the stockade; she had learned
to reach up with her trunk to the stockade machans.
Our machan was firmly built into the branches of the
tree. I was glad of that. Most of them hang dizzily out
from the bare trunk, slung from iron stays fixed to
the tree by spikes.

The elephants came out in three sections, rushing,
not stopping at the water edge, right out into the
deep crossing. Frannie and I, while snapping frantically, watched anxiously for the baby. He wasn't
with the first section. There was a tiny one with the
second section, but Frannie said no, it wasn't ours. I
watched it, wee thing, bravely swimming, its little
head a black, bobbing dot in the water getting further
and further left behind by the big ones. Oh, baby,
baby! But just then, as though at last the dam had
burst, the final section, the main herd with the big

bulls, came tumbling out with a roar, an avalanche of
bodies, big and little, in a rolling cloud of dust.

Last of all the enormous tusker, tail up and prodigious stride, as though hell were after him, and at his heels, our baby, running and running with all its little might, so tiny. 'Oh, big Daddy, here I am. I'm coming. Don't forget me.' They struck the water, and as they struck it their trumpeting became a tremendous roar. Cape said it was wonderful to hear in the microphone. They struck out to swim. Baby, oh baby, striking out after them, so terribly little. By the time he had struggled to midstream, the herd was over.

And for agonized minutes we watched the little thing struggling, dazed, going round and round in circles, expecting every instant to see it go under. Frannie shrieked: 'Save the baby!' I shrieked. Barbie, on the other side of the river, was crying. For you just can't imagine how lovable the wee things are. Then a raft came gliding toward the wee head, the little creature was seized by the ear, and half on the raft, half in the water, held up by a rope around its body, it was towed across to the far shore. A great shout went up and waving of torches from our side. The baby, exhausted, lay in a snug nest of sand and
slept. Two watchers stayed by it. Early in the evening the mother came down and took the baby away. And so ended our keddah.

EPILOGUE

Mysore City,
March.

I wish I could tell you how beautiful Mysore is, *Patriarchal*
and what a serene, lovely atmosphere broods over a *Utopia*
ravishing landscape and over the lovely city itself, like
a spiritual benediction. For me (perhaps I imagine it,
though others acknowledge it, too) it emanates from
the glowing ruby light on the highest and noblest of
the flood-lit palace domes. It is the very heart of a man,
the ruler, the Maharajah; the glowing beacon means
his presence here in his city watching over his people.
I never thought to live in patriarchal times—to go so
far back in history—to experience a patriarchal
Utopia. But everything here has something of the
magic and poetry of legend in it.

We have been writing our story, re-writing it. For
three weeks we have done nothing else. It has been a
hard task—has torn our combined brains to tatters

133

and drained them white—such an effort—really terrific. But we are pleased with the result. The mould is finally cast; now to give it life.

If we do it well, the film will have something in it of this quality of legend and deep natural mystery. You see, the great natural spectacle in our story was to be a wild elephant drive into a 'keddah' stockade—regular whoopee.

Elephant Dance Our drive came off splendidly, our captured herd was a magnificent one. We let them go again and took pictures of them coming and going. When we saw our 'rushes' a miracle appeared on the screen—no semblance of a drive, but instead these most extraordinary creatures, as if in the heart of their mysterious jungle, 'going places'. Where were they going? Why, to the Elephant Dance, of course, just as it is in Kipling's story. So we re-wove our story all round this elephant dance. All we need to complete the illusion is their feet in action. All our camp of twenty-five tame elephants has gone into training like a ballet chorus—to learn to dance. Isn't it a quaint life?

So now that our script is beyond the peradventure of further change, we can go ahead with our work as fast as possible. Our Kala-Nag has gone 'musth' again. But still we talk of going back in May, on the Italian Line—the only one on which we can hope to get passage at short notice.

The whole Indian adventure has been a fairy story.

134

[*facing* 'PFUI, KALA NAG, WHAT DIRTY EARS!']

There is magic in the very air, and the beauty of it acts like a drug—a timeless dream. No one has painted or sung it adequately, because it seems to be inexpressible.

Postscript, London, Feb'y 14th, '37.

So many people ask me what has happened to Sabu. As I write he is here in London, he and his older brother and a Hindu tutor, living in a hotel near the British Museum. He is very happy. Every time I see him I ask him, 'Aren't you homesick, Sabu? Aren't you tired of London?' But he answers with always the same smile on his lips, the same light in his eyes. People stop him in the streets and ask, 'Is this the Elephant Boy?' They know him from his pictures in the papers.

He does not speak English readily because he does not speak much anyway. He likes to come to our house and turn on the radio. In our compound in Mysore he played an instrument, like a harp, called a bulbul tharang; he would play it day and night, passionately, until someone stopped him. He and Sultan, another little boy from the Palace stables, gave concerts together; Sultan did singing and pantomime and never failed to bring down the house. Sabu has sent to India for his bulbul tharang.

We brought him to London because there was work for him still to do on the picture in the studio.

135

There was dialogue. And for six weeks through the whole night, in the penetrating cold misty nights on the banks of the Colne, he worked in nothing but his dhoti (loin-cloth), evidently suffering no cold. Not a sniffle has he had all this winter so far in London.

The studio went wild about him. His acting amazed them; they called him a genius. They insured his life for £50,000 and set their best writer to work writing for him the story for another film.

But in the meantime our own picture through months of work in the studio has steadily been mounting and mounting—soaring—into the realm of 'big' productions. And Sabu must carry it all. Either we have been led by our enthusiasm for the boy into a great mistake, or we shall have judged rightly and Sabu will carry the film to success.

The first night, the London première, will come. (Yes, Sabu will be there.) And then, as the film unfolds, the miracle must happen—Sabu must capture his audience, and the audience must—or will it?—take the little Indian boy to its heart.